TABLE OF

MW00711902

<u>101 INSPIRATIONAL POEMS</u>

Rev. Christopher Ervin writes inspirational poems, speaks at Inspirational Seminars, and preaches the Gospel, attempting to reach the lost and the saved, with one message, "There is Victory through Jesus Christ! He is also available for Public Engagements and Poetry Readings, and has readily available audio tapes of his poetry which he dramatically reads with inspiring background music.

Please call (404)668-3355 for more information, or write us at:
God In Action Publications Inc.,
881 North Ave N.W
Atlanta, GA 30318

Published by God In Action Publications
881 North Avenue N.W.
Atlanta, GA 30318

www.Victoryinsight.com

Printed in the United States of America
By Bob and Jean of Minute Man Press
Mableton, Georgia

Library of Congress Cataloging-in-Publication Data

Copy write: 1987 Library of Congress TXU 278 130, 315 772, 472 130

Victory in Sight Copy Write 2005

Christopher Ervin/Poetry for the world

ISBN 09766 769-0-7

References:

DEDICATION
To my family in life,
To my family in Christ,
To those who truly seek,
To those who want to know,
To those who truly believe,
And to those who want to grow,
this book is for you.

Visit our Web site at:
www.Victoryinsight.com

A special thanks to my wife Daphine.
To my mother Minnie Ervin, my sisters Jean and Cathy in Cleveland Ohio, all of our families and friends in life and in Christ.
Reverend Anthony A. W. Motley, Pastor, Lindsay Street Baptist Church, Atlanta Georgia, where I have served the past 11 years as a Senior Associate Minister, and proudly continue to serve.
Special thanks to my editor Jennifer Church.
My attorney Steven Kiser.
All of the ministers too numerous to name who have blessed me with their ministries, and continue to do so.
To my cousin Victor Ervin who assisted me with the cover and design.

I thank everyone, for your love and your support.

7 STEPS TO HEALTH, HAPPINESS & SUCCESS!
THROUGH BIBLICAL PASSAGES

7 STEPS
TO HEALTH, HAPPINESS, & SUCCESS
THROUGH BIBLICAL PASSAGES

Some year's ago, at a youth conference I attended, someone asked the question, "Are there certain steps people can take to assure their success?" The counselor answered, "It depends on what you would define as success. For many years I pondered that question, in my personal quest for success While success to some, can be found in the form of financial wealth, to others is the simple satisfaction of living a simple and comfortable life, and yet still to others it can be much, much more, or less. My personal philosophy of success is one, which I adopted shortly after reading Stephen R. Covey's, "7 Habits of Highly Effective People", and my motivation for the 7 Steps to Health Happiness, and success. My personal philosophy of success, is that when die, at my eulogy, I would like it said that I did all that I could to lift the name of Jesus Christ, to lift up my brothers and sisters in Christ, to help and to motivate the poor, less fortunate and poverty stricken, and to do the right thing; and finally, that I was a charitable and giving man. To me, that is the essence of success! My Father, Benjamin F. Ervin, was the essence of a successful man in that he served God, his family, and his church, all the days of his life. The greatest gift that my mother Minnie who now resides in Cleveland Ohio, and my father who is now with Christ, gave to my sisters and I, was introducing us to Jesus Christ and the church at an early age. When I attended his funeral, many came with inspiring testimonies about his life, how he served the church as a senior deacon, how he served his family, friends, relatives, and community. I was hard for me to accept the fact that I had lost him, but I found solace in knowing that we would meet and greet one another again, through the grace of Jesus Christ. To me that is success, to know that when I leave, my life will have meant something to someone other than myself.

In formulating "Victory In Sight", I've incorporated some biblical passages to assist the Christian walk in health, happiness, and success. While these steps and passages are not the only keys to gaining all of the above, they are major avenues for those seeking the right and straight way. I'd like to thank Rev. Anthony A. W. Motley, my great friend, counselor, and Pastor for all he has done to assist me in my growth and service to Christ. Rev. Motley Pastors the Lindsay Street Baptist Church in Atlanta Georgia, where I have served for over the past 10 years, and continue to serve, as a Senior Associate Minister under his great leadership. Special thanks, to my wife Daphine, for her love, and support of my ministry and the multi numerous projects that I am constantly tasked with in and of the service of the Kingdom of God. I'd also like to thank my mother, Minnie L. Ervin, for her leadership and guidance in my life. I truly must thank my mother and my father for being examples, for my sisters Jean, Cathy, Ann and I to follow, and for them introducing us to Jesus Christ, knowing that with Christ, the victory is truly insight.

2a.

STEP I
FEAR THE LORD THY GOD
PSALMS 128

"How blessed is everyone who fear's the Lord, who walks in His ways. When you shall eat the fruit of your hands, you will be happy and it will be well with you. Your wife shall be like a fruitful vine, within your house, your children like olive plants around your table. Behold, for thus shall the man be blessed, who fears the Lord. The Lord bless you from Zion, and may you see the prosperity of Jerusalem all the days of your life. Indeed, may you see your children's, children. Peace be upon Israel!"

In Proverbs 14:27, it says that the fear of the Lord is a fountain of life, that one may avoid the snares of death. And we, as a people know, as history has continued to show, that we do not go against that which we fear, because we can easily predict the consequences. Moses loved the Lord, and feared the Lord, and followed the Lord. As a result God saved a nation. Do you not feel that he would do the same for all of his people who fear, love and follow? It is said, that out of mankind's fears, come mankind's actions. I can assure you today that Satan does not fear the Lord, and that is why our world is so plagued with poverty, war, crime, and disease. A person who knows God, fears and follows Him, knowing of His infinite power, is a successful person. It takes a person fearful of God, to do the right thing in our society today, for living within Gods law is our guarantee of success! Fear the Lord thy God and love the Lord with all your heart and you'll find that you do things differently, and that you are God In Action, for God is in action through you. You'll also find that success was always yours you simply needed to claim it, when you named Jesus Christ as your personal Lord and Savior. Fearing God will make you strong, for you shall not fear man, but the maker of man. You shall not fear challenges, for you shall know that all battles God has and shall continue to win. You shall rise and not falter, and you shall stay near the Altar, for you know the power of prayer, and the reason you do fear, our God. You shall walk with your head high, and not let your spirit die, for you walk in the presence of the Lord, and you walk in the presence of Divinity. If you serve our God who is omnipotent, than what does that make you? Surely, if you walk with the great, than you have a bit of that greatness within you. Know who you are; and claim the victory, when you claim Christ!

3a.

STEP II
PUT ON GOD'S COAT OF ARMOR
EPHESIANS 6:11

"*Put on the whole armor of God, that you may be able to stand firm against the schemes of the devil.* Stand firm therefore, having **girded your loins with truth**, and having put on the **breastplate of righteousness**, and having **shod your feet with the preparation of the gospel of peace**, in addition to all, taking up **the shield of faith with which you will be able to extinguish all the flaming missiles of the evil one.** And take the **Helmut of salvation, and the sword of the spirit, which is the word of God.**"

When we put on God's whole coat of armor, no evil may befall us, because we stand strong, as warriors, able to overcome any obstacle, which confronts us. It is important for us as Christians today to remain focused, and in our armor at all times, because the devil is a busy liar, and is always waiting for us to drop our shields. Don't drop your shield, always wear your armor, and success, you are sure to find.

Let's for a moment examine God's coat of armor, which will help us to be successful in everything we do.

A. Gird your loins with truth. A popular saying which also comes from biblical reading is, 'the truth shall set you free." Remember the devil is a liar, and truth shall always overshadow anything evil throws at you. Truth is what Gods laws are based on. Truth is the principle that our Father tells us to live by. And truth is one of the greatest forms of love there is, by truth we measure everything our society today is based on. Keep the truth, and you will keep God in your life.

B. Breastplate of Righteousness. If we are true to God, and true to one another, we will be righteous in the sight of our fellow brothers and sisters, more so we will be righteous in God' s sight. A breast plate was one of the most important pieces of armor a soldier would use before battle because it was used to shield the body from incoming articles and weapons. Today righteousness is as important in our society as it has always been. Thank God for his righteous people, it is because of their truth and love that our society has come as far as it has today and righteousness shall determine how far we as a nation will go in the future.

C. Shod your feet with the preparation to the gospel of peace. I can still remember that as a child, there were many times that I attempted to walk barefoot in the park or while visiting relatives in the South. I was never able to do it, because my feet were not accustomed to walking with out the support and protection of a sandal or shoe. In order for Christians to walk in truth and in righteousness, we must first be prepared thru the understanding of Gods words and ways that our Father in Heaven would have us to go. Likewise it is impossible for mankind to continually gain in society without preparation and study. Shod your feet my brothers and sisters with the preparation of the gospel of Jesus Christ, which is the true Gospel of truth, of righteousness, and of love. I now know and understand that the reason people are able to walk barefoot in the South is because they had become accustomed to doing so as children, and as they grew older their feet grew stronger. So it is with Christ my friends, the more you walk in His precious light, the stronger and more prepared you become to walk in life. Never shod your foot wear, be prepared, and you shall walk with the most high!

D. The shield of faith. The shield is another most important piece of armor no soldier could survive without it! How else could you retract arrows and missiles formed to destroy you with out a shield? Likewise my brothers and sisters, with out faith we have no course for the battle. A verse in Hebrews I always refer to is Hebrews 11:1-2. Now faith is the substance of things hoped for, the evidence of things not seen. For by it the elders obtained a good testimony. Without faith it is impossible to win against Satan. With out faith it is impossible for us to win, because if there were no faith there would be no cause. How great is your faith? How great is your success? Without faith Moses would not have been able to lead the Israelites into freedom. Without faith David could not have conquered Goliath. Without faith Jews and African Americans could not have conquered slavery, and without faith, where would America be today? Remember, you cannot succeed at anything in life, without faith, in yourself, and in God. Keep the faith, and success you will surely find.

E. The Helmut of Salvation and the Sword of the Spirit which is the word of God. Everyone knows that the head is the most important part of our body; in war soldiers are taught that when you attack the head first, the body will follow. Thank God for our head which shall never fail us. Christ is our head and our Salvation. Through His death and resurrection we obtained life everlasting. Christ is our only Salvation; if it were not for Christ this world would not be what it is today. And if it were not for Christ, this world could not be what it's going to be tomorrow. As a matter of fact if there were no Christ I am very doubtful that we would be here today. Thank God for the Salvation we've obtained through His loving Son. My mother, use to tell me growing up as a child that it is important to get as much knowledge as possible. She wasn't just speaking of educational knowledge. She was speaking of Biblical knowledge and the word of God. No other book, no other words will ever match the power, truth and effectiveness of the word of God. No other book can guide and lead and strengthen, such as the word of God. No other book can pick you up, and take you where you know you need to be, than the word of God. Through His word is Power, through his spirit is power. Through the book of God, is all the power you will ever need. It will take you anywhere and help you to be, all you can be. It will enlighten your life, and help you to see. It will guarantee your success! Read Gods Holy word and success I'm sure you'll find! One more thing to remember, when you read Gods word, you'll begin to act and speak in Gods way. Your mouth shall utter prayers and words you did not know where in you. You will speak with high authority, for Gods authority will be in you. You shall pray a little different, speak to your friends and loved ones a little differently, and God shall guide your words, for the word of God will be in you, in your heart, in your mind, and in your body. And remember the word of God is your greatest weapon in battling Satan, and your greatest asset, in accomplishing anything in Life. God's word is your sword in battling Satan. With Gods weapon which is His word, you shall win every time. Carry it with you and watch Satan run, but don't just carry the physical book, carry Gods words in your heart, in your mind, and in your soul, and if you do that simple thing, you'll find your always in control. Remember to be a soldier in Christ Army is our greatest role.

STEP V
YOU ARE WHAT YOU EAT
GENESIS 1:11-12

"*Then God said, "Let the earth sprout vegetarian, plants yielding seed after their kind, and trees bearing fruit with seed in them after their kind," and God saw it was good. In the book of Leviticus 11: 1-47, God spoke to Moses and Aaron, saying to them, "This is the kind of creature you may eat from among all the animals that are on the land. He also did so with all the creatures that are in the water, amongst the birds, amongst the insects, and finally God tells them what carcass they would defile themselves with, by eating. I would encourage everyone to read Leviticus, and rightly divide the word of God."*

A proper diet plan in today's society is almost impossible. With so many food groups to choose from the food industry has become a multi-trillion dollar industry. That notwithstanding; food born illnesses and disease throughout the world has increased steadily over the past decade, now reaching phenomenal levels. In order for people to maintain healthy bodies and minimize sickness, doctors and specialist of all backgrounds are recommending specialized diets and eating habits at new record levels. People are turning to Atkins and South Beach formulas to control weight, and proper eating habits. I believe that if we would like to remain as healthy as possible, we need to keep one popular phrase in mind, "You are what you eat". If you remember those five simple words, and keep active lives, I am sure that God will continue to bless you in all that you do. Remember that our bodies are the temple of God. God does not want anything in the body that would corrupt or bring shame to His name. When the Pagans over ran the church, which is a part of the body of Christ, Christ became angered and ran them from with in. Likewise so we must run foreign obstacles from our bodies. Another saying which has proven to be correct, is, "Cleanliness, is next to Godliness". Always remember to wash your hands and foods thoroughly, for we kill germs and disease in so doing. A serve safe rule everyone should know, "never eat foods or attempt to keep foods that have been out for more than four hours." It would be impossible for me to go up against some of the most leading nutritionist today and debate on what is good and what is bad as far as food substances, and drugs for our bodies. As one who has Asthma, I would be the last to attempt to direct anyone on proper health or eating habits, however let us remember the words of Christ.

Christ said, *"Where two or more are gathered in my name, there I am also"*. Let us pray together that God will intercede for us in these times of trouble. Let us pray that God frees us from the disease and pain that Satan and mankind have inflicted upon us, through their poor production and failure to properly educate our society of the positive as well as negatives, of our food supply right here in America.

The old church members remember the lines from a song which we still sing today, "God is my medicine, and God has my cure, God is my all and all!" Thank God that our God is God, and can make any wrong thing right. Let us continue to pray for one another that our God continues to enlighten us and guide us in terms of how we eat and care for our bodies. If we are healthy we are healthy through the grace of God. We help God keep us healthy by properly taking care of our bodies, and continue to offer them as living sacrifices for His Kingdom.

STEP VI
BE YE GENEROUS!
PROVERBS 11:25

"*The generous man will be prosperous, and he who waters will himself be watered.* Proverbs 2:1-29; "*A good name is to be more desired than great riches, favor is better than silver and gold. The rich and the poor have a common bond, that the Lord is the maker of them all. He who is generous will be blessed, for he gives some of his food to the poor.*"

One of my favorite scriptures that my father taught me as a child is, "*Cast thy bread upon the water and thy shall find it after many days.*" To this day, as I learn and continue to grow in Christ, one thing I know is that, that which we give in the name of Christ we receive back in greater abundance. It is said that happiness comes in different shapes, forms and sizes, how one measures it, is largely dependent on how one views life in general. I don't know about you, but since I've found Jesus, I've found health, happiness, the true meaning of success, and I shall dwell in the house of the lord forever! Malachi 3:812, "*Will a man rob God? Yet ye have robbed me. But you say, Wherein have we robbed thee? In tithes and offerings. You are cursed with a curse: for you have robbed me, even this whole nation. Bring all the tithes into the storehouse, that there may be meat in mine house, and prove me now, saith the Lord of hosts, if I will not open you the windows of heaven and pour you out a blessing, that there shall not be room enough to receive it. And I will rebuke the devourer for your sakes, and he shall not destroy the fruits of your ground; neither shall your vine cast her fruit before the time in the field, saith the Lord of hosts. And all nations shall call you blessed: for you shall be a delightful land, saith the Lord of hosts.*" This final chapter of the Old Testament says it all, that we must give to God first, because God gave to us first, and gave His only begotten Son. So many people today are betting on the lottery or a law suit to get them where they feel they need to be financially, and in doing so they make the lottery and those things their Idols. God said that I am a jealous God, and thou shall have no other Gods before me.

Another thing I'd like to leave with you is, "only what you do for Christ shall last!" Christ when speaking to His Disciples often spoke of giving from the heart, He said, when you do for the least of these, you do for me. A rich man once asked Christ how he could get into heaven and receive the blessings of God, Jesus told him to give up his wealth, for it would be easier for a camel to come thru an eye of a needle, than it would be for him to get into Heaven.

11a.

Today we live in a society where ones economic value determines ones Socio-economical status. Our society is so caught up in becoming rich and famous that we often forget and neglect one another in our daily strides to become one of the above. And yet when we look around at third world countries, and yes even in our own back yards in America, the so called land of the free, the poverty level continues to escalate, while our neighbors and children are dying in record numbers from drug abuse, lack of food, education, Medicare, and crime abuse, just to name a few of the daily struggles that our own brothers and sisters must battle daily. I can only ask, America, where is your shame? While we give hundreds and thousands, and yes, even millions of dollars yearly to other countries, we give not nearly enough to conquer and defeat poverty in our own backyards. I am in no way attempting to degrade this country which I love and serve, however we need a serious awakening, and we need to look to our God who helped us to make this country what it was yesterday, what it can be tomorrow. What made this country what is was, was what our late great President John F. Kennedy once said in one of his greatest speeches, "Ask not what your country can do for you, but what you can do for your country." Our country became great because it was a country of giving, and we gave from the heart.

STEP VII
DON'T GROW WEARY!
GALATIANS 6:9

"And let us not lose heart in doing good, for in due time we shall reap if we do not grow weary. "

In writing, "Victory In Sight", I wanted to inspire men, women and children alike, to grow closer in their personal walk with God. More so I wanted to inspire my fellow Christians to keep the faith and not to lose hope in this, sometimes distressing world in which we live. Many times while watching the news and seeing all that's going on in the world today, it becomes easy to see why there is so much negativism throughout our society. The Bible tells us to wait on the Lord, to hang on in there, to persevere, and not give in. Through continued prayer, the constant inspiring of each other and continued growth in the word of God, we can overcome all things through Christ, which is in us. We must be as athletes, constantly conditioning our minds and bodies for success through Christ. If we do these things then truly victory shall be ours. If you know of someone about to throw in the towel, ask them to read Matthew 6:19-34, and remember verse 33, *"SEEK FIRST HIS KINGDOM, AND HIS RIGHEOUSNESS, AND ALL THESE THINGS SHALL BE ADDED TO YOU."*

Let us also remember the one thing God reminds us we must have if we are to ward off Satan's missiles, and that is the shield of faith. For truly we walk by faith and not by sight. Remember through faith, Moses freed a people, through faith David destroyed a giant, through faith Meshach, Shadrach, and Abednego, with stood the fiery flames of the King. Through faith Daniel slept quietly and lived overnight in a Lions Den, and through faith my brothers and sisters you too, can truly say I have the victory, because I have Christ.

In closing my brothers and sisters I ask that you read the book of Joshua. Joshua was called by God to take over leading his people. He had a hard act to follow, after all Moses was a seasoned leader, a proven leader, and a leader well respected. Joshua needed a recipe for success, for the mission God had given him was considered by most a mission impossible. If you look closely at the book of Joshua you will find that the recipe God gave Joshua is included in the Seven Steps you have just read.

Joshua 1:7 *"Be strong and very courageous, that you may observe to do according to all the law which Moses My servant commanded you, do not turn from it to the right hand or to the left, that you may prosper wherever you go. 8 This book of the law shall not depart from your mouth, but you shall meditate upon it day and night, that you may observe to do according to all that is written in it, for then you will make your way prosperous, and then you will have good success. Have I not commanded you? Be strong and of good courage; do not be afraid, nor be dismayed, for the Lord your God is with you wherever you go."*

Finally I must quote Isaiah 40:31 *"But they that wait upon the Lord shall renew their strength; they shall mount up with wings as eagles; they shall run and not be weary; and they shall walk; and not be faint. Wait upon the Lord my brothers and sisters, and as sure as He saved Israel, He will surely come your way! "*

Remember my brothers and sisters, that wherever you go, take Christ with you, and you shall choose the right roads. May God bless, May God Keep you, and May God be with you, wherever you go!

SUMMIZATION OF THE SEVEN STEPS

In summarizing the Seven Steps listed on the previous pages, I simply ask that you look closely at the book of Joshua 1: 1-10. Here we find that Joshua has been called after the death of Moses to lead his people over Jordan to the land, which God had promised them. This was an incredible mission that was given to Joshua, who was not a seasoned leader as Moses. Now in this book we find that Joshua was called to lead millions of people, and he was a bit challenged by this most awesome task given to him. What Joshua needed was a recipe, ingredient, or a formula of sorts, and what some today would classify as a game plan. I want you to know my brothers and sisters that when God calls you, God gives you all you need to accomplish anything in life. In this book Joshua, is given several ingredients by God, as he went forth in the leadership of Gods people. 1. Be Strong and courageous, because you will lead these people to inherit the land I swore to their forefathers to give to them. 2. Be careful to obey all the law my servant Moses gave you; do not turn from it to the right or to the left, that you may be successful wherever you go. 3. Do not let this book of the Law depart from your mouth; meditate on it day and night; so that you may be careful to do everything written in it, then you will be prosperous and successful.

Joshua remained strong and courageous, as the Lord had commanded, he obeyed all of the Laws which God had given him, he did not turn from those Laws, from the left, nor the right; he meditated on God's words, and never let those words depart from his mouth. And finally he kept His faith in God and the promises of God and as a result he was prosperous and successful in leading his people over the Jordan.

As Christians today if we follow God as commanded of us, if we keep His words and Laws close to our hearts and minds, and finally my brothers and sisters, if we keep the faith, God promises us prosperity, and success to us all. Remember with and through God all things are possible, and only what you do for Christ will last. Claim the victory today, when you claim Christ as your personal Savior. My prayer is that God keep and bless you all, as he blesses a field of lilies, forever, and ever. Amen.

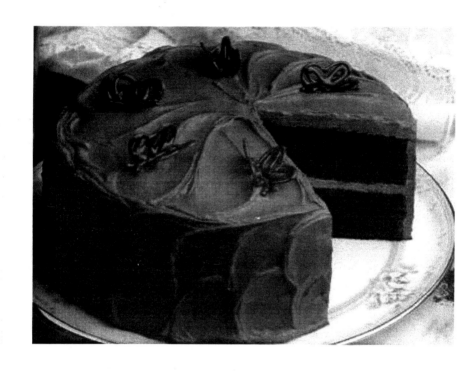

JUST AS YOU NEED A RECIPE TO MAKE A CAKE, YOU NEED A RECIPE FOR SUCCESS, AND THAT RECIPE, IS IN THE WORD OF GOD!

SOME WHO'VE INSPIRED THE AUTHOR

When I think of inspiration, I think of people who I have and have not met in my walk in life, that have had an effect and impact in my train of thought. More so I would like to thank these people, for their leadership and the inspiration which they have provided for not only myself, but for countless others. There are many others, other than the number of people who you shall see on the following pages which have helped to inspire me in my walk in life, and they are too numerous to mention all of them in this book. So I've included a few I've be fortunate enough to meet, who still today are on the battle fields of life, pressing on with Victory in Sight! Whatever you do in life, wherever you go, remember one thing: Only what we do for Christ will last!

Distributed by CASI, Yonkers, N.Y. The Giving Hand © 1997 STAPCO

Oprah Winfrey. Oprah Winfrey has and continues to inspire millions around the world. Her gifts have not only reached millions in America, but millions in Africa and all around the world, a true philanthropist. It is said that you can measure the success of a leader, by the amount they give back. One of my favorite songs is, "You can't beat Gods Giving, no matter how you try. The more you give, the more He gives to you, so just keep on giving, because it's really true. You can't beat God's giving, no matter how you try." Thank you Oprah, you have given and continue to give back, of that you've been blessed with. Though I have not met you, you are an inspiration to me and my family. You continue to lift those less fortunate and you do so not seeking accolades from your peers. Thank You.

Rev. Anthony A. W. Motley. My friend, my Pastor, and fellow advocate of Christ. This charismatic leader has been Pastor of Lindsay Street Baptist Church for more than 24 years. He continues to be a vital asset not only to the church but to the entire community which he is dedicated to rebuilding. Truly when I look to this awesome leader who is also President of the New Era Baptist Convention, I think of the Apostle Paul, always seeking to lift his people in the victorious name of Jesus Christ! Truly I would not be who I am today as a minister and servant of God, if it were not for my friend and Pastor Rev. Anthony A. W. Motley!

Dr. Joseph E. Lowery. One of the greatest moments in my life, was the day I met this awesome leader of God. Dr. Lowery has done so much for the civil rights of not just African Americans, but for the civil rights of all people throughout the world. I am proud to say I know him as a friend and advocate of Christ. Our church is so blessed to have him speak yearly at our men's conference. He usually reminds us before he begins speaking that our church is located on Joseph E. Lowery Blvd. Personally I believe he dissevers much more than a street in his name. Dr. Lowery will go down in history as a forefront runner and drum major of justice and peace for all! What a true testament of victory!

Andrew Young. What can you say about Andrew Young? Statesman, Businessman, Humanitarian. He is known around the world for his participation with Dr. Martin Luther King and countless other's in the Non-Violent Freedom Movement. An ordained minister, he served as president of the National Council of Churches in 2000-2001, among countless other roles, and was responsible for bringing Atlanta, Georgia to the forefront of this great nation. Author of, "A Way Out of No Way", and "An Easy Burden", Andrew continues to be a vital asset to the growth and development of this great nation. Truly a man who has and continues to inspire me and countless others in and around this great nation!

Charles Barkley. When you talk about a big man, don't forget to talk about Charles Barkley. This superstar, mesmerized us for years with his performances in the NBA. These days Charles is a frequent commentator on various sport networks, and is a prominent businessman as well. Charles Barkley has always been known for speaking out, and I can only salute him for speaking his mind and speaking the truths on real issues which affect our nation. A truly inspiring man and leader!

Jamie Foxx. Today when you think about Jamie Foxx, think Oscar! Recently Jamie Foxx became the Third African American to win the Oscar for Best Actor, and if you saw the movie you would of voted too! Jamie is a man who can make you laugh and a man who can make you cry! Several stellar performances escalated this inspiring figure from comedy to serious screen acting, and if that's not enough he can sing too! God sure gifted Jamie, and Jamie is sure sharing his gift with the world. Thanks Jaime, we're sure there's more to come!

M.C. Hammer. Hammer Time! Anyone who knows music must know M. C. Hammer. It takes a great man to talk about his ups and downs, but an even greater man to get back up and continue his climb. M. C. Hammer is back, and will continue to be a positive influence to millions of Americans. An accomplished actor, Hammer also appears on numerous Trinity Broadcasting Programs, lifting up the name of Jesus Christ! A man who has lifted so many, deserves to be lifted!

Bishop T. D. Jakes. Known all over the world as a true leader in the ministry of Jesus Christ. T. D. Jakes continues as a major leader and contributor in the building of the Kingdom of Christ right here on earth. T. D. Jakes uses every gift he has for the building of Gods Kingdom. As a Pastor, Evangelist, book writer, song and movie writer and producer, you may ask the question, "What else can and does he do?" T. D. Jakes has proved to me that beyond a shadow of a doubt, when you build with God, He will pour you out blessing which you won't have room enough to receive! A true General in God's Army, he will continue to be blessed in all he does!

Jimmy Johnson. Someone asked me the question, "why does this man always smile!" I answered, "if you were as successful as he, you would always smile too!" Gaining his fame in taking the Dallas Cowboys to two back to back Super Bowl Championships, this man is a true leader, both on and off the field. A God fearing man and a great leader, today you can usually catch Jimmy commentating many NFL games. Jimmy also speaks around the world, inspiring men and women from all walks of life. A true and Victorious leader.

Ozzie Davis. If you don't know Ozzie Davis, then you've never watched television. Ozzie has blessed us over the century and more with his skills and meaningful roles in the movies. Its an honor to say I've had the honor of meeting and sharing the company of such an icon! He and his wife Ruby Dee are jewels in Gods Kingdom, and have truly blessed millions in their too numerous to name all, performances on stage and in films. But Ozzie didn't stop their, he was also involved in the Civil Rights Movements. Truly a Victorious and God fearing man! Two weeks prior to going to press with this book I learned of Ozzie's death. It was said that he died quietly in his sleep. This great man will be loved, cherished and greatly missed, but his spirit will always survive! Ozzie Davis a man who has truly inspired myself and millions, and will continue to do so through his many great works

Congressman John Lewis. I thought I knew Congressman Lewis from what I had learned of his marching and work with Dr. Martin Luther King and the Civil Rights Movement. But then I read his Book, "Walking With The Wind", and I became even more inspired by this truly inspiring and dedicated to the American people leader. Untarnished as most politicians today, God is at the head of his life, and that is why he has been and continues to be so successful and loved by the world! Great work Congressman Lewis, please don't ever stop!

Hershel Walker. Growing up one of my favorite Television Hero's was Superman. And then when I got into Football, there was Hershel Walker! If you want to know the story of a truly victorious individual, talk to Hershel Walker. A Heisman Trophy winner as a junior in college, in 1986 he entered the NFL leading the league in rushing and became an All-Pro. His philosophy, "Run the race against yourself and not the guy in the other lane," is inspiring to people everywhere. A moving speaker, he enjoys the opportunity to share his message of Victory to audiences everywhere! I truly do not know of many men like Hershel; so sincere and so real. Now a very successful businessman with a food chain that continues to grow, Hershel is the essence of a truly victorious individual, with God at the helm of his ship!

XIII

Senator David Scott. Senator David Scott has been running the race in Politics for more than 28 years in the state of Georgia. During my first run as a radio talk show host in Atlanta Georgia, Senator Scott gave me my first real interview and an opportunity to learn why he is such a popular leader and inspirational figure for the thousands of Georgians he has proudly served over the past 28 years in the U.S. Government. Not just an elegant leader, but a educated, dedicated, and determined leader of the people. God has blessed this gracious leader, and I truly believe that Senator David Scott will continue to bless the citizens of Georgia, for many years to come. I look up to this man as an inspirational figure, because of his open and notated contributions to not only Georgians but to the world! Senator Scott, we need more leaders like you.

The Honorable Mayor Shirley Franklin. I truly know that I have been blessed, because I can truly say that I know and have seen a real leader, and a real mover and shaker in action. However, the big plus is that this moving leader is a true God fearing and God loving, mover and shaker! If you look at the success of Atlanta, Georgia today. No doubt you will see Shirley Franklin the cities' Mayor behind the continued success of this great and growing city in the south. Monthly she meets with the Interfaith Leaders in the communities and gives them the bottom line in the effort to deal with those least among us! Please note that this is what Christ told his Disciples, *"When you do the least for these among us, you do for me!"* What a Mayor, a Mayor who truly cares! This is a servant and a leader who will continue to climb!

Thomas W. Dortch Jr. Chairman of 100 Black Men of America's National Board of Directors, and President and Chief Executive Officer of TWD, Inc. Thomas has been my friend and mentor for many years. I consider myself to be blessed to know him and his family. This inspiring leader continues to provide leadership and direction throughout communities around the world. As author of, "The Miracles of Mentoring: The Joy of Investing in Our Future," published by Doubleday Books, Tommy as I like to call him, gives us an in dept focus on mentoring the youths of America. When I think of Tommy, I again think of the words of Jesus Christ, "When you do for the least of these, you do for me. If you meet him, you will easily see why this charismatic leader has been and continues to be so successful and an inspiration to multitudes!

Dr. Martin Luther King Jr. Though he's gone, his spirit still survives, in the hearts of men and women, and in all of our lives. This man has inspired me to become who I am today in Christ. This Christ like prophet's contribution's to the world in my opinion has been unparallel to most of our leaders of today and in the past. To be like him is one of my greatest inspirations. Dr. Martin Luther King, was a master mind!

Minnie L. Ervin. When I think and talk about inspirational leadership, I could not leave out the one who brought me first to know the name of Jesus Christ. My mother has always ushered me to keep up the good fight, and to stay focused on my service to God! I thank God for the leadership she has given my sisters and I, and for making sure, as we grew up, we grew up with Jesus Christ in our lives! It truly makes a difference to know Jesus!

Gavin MacLeod. You may of known him as the character Murray from the Mary Tyler Moore Show, but to most this man for many years was known as Captain Merrill Stubing, the lead character of, Love Boat", the popular television series which ran consecutively from the late 1970's through 1986. The series was so popular even today people are still watching the re-runs and talking about it. The series has also been said to be responsible for the popularity of Cabin Cruise Ships in America and around the world today. This born again Christian, has definitely been a great inspiration to me, and to quote him, 'I look a little like Ted Lange', one of his Co Stars, who played the popular character of Isaac the bartender during the show's run.

Xenona Clayton. What a gem! A true Pioneer who worked closely with Martin Luther King Jr. while employed with the Southern Christian Leadership Conference. In 1967, she became the first Black person in the South to host her own television show called, The Xernona Clayton Show." To top off her astonishing career, Mrs. Clayton also is the Founder and Producer of The Trumpet Awards, which recognizes the outstanding contributions of African Americans around the world. This lavish event is held each year in Atlanta Georgia, and if your blessed to attend once, you'll definitely want to come again. As my friend, I thank Mrs. Clayton for all the inspiration she has provided to me, in my quest to give back that which God has blessed me with.

If anyone where to ask me how did I get to where I am today? I would tell them that God blessed me with a God fearing mother and father. Above is my father **Benjamin F. Ervin**, who has gone on to be with the Lord and my mother **Minnie** who you've seen on a previous page and who even today, continues to assist me in the direction of my ministry. One thing I have learned from my parents that I am truly thankful for is, "only what you do for Christ will last." "We are all just travelers here in this world for only a short while, but the good news is, through Jesus Christ, we have eternal life with God!"

My wife **Daphine** and I have found great inspiration through our grandson **Alija,** and we always will find time to spend with him, preparing him and developing him for the world ahead.   As you can see, Alija already knows a bit about victory! Isn't it something how children can inspire and provide motivation?   Our sincere prayer and focus is that Alija accepts Christ at an early age and that he will dwell in the house of the Lord, forever!

Vince Dooley. What a success story from a man who truly knows victory! Vince coached the University of Georgia football team (the Bulldogs) for twenty-five years, leading them to the 1980 National Championship. He served as UGA's Athletic Director from 1979 to 2003, overseeing the rise of Georgia's athletic program to one of the nations finest! Vince Dooley a God fearing and truly victorious leader.

Brett Pulley: Editor: Forbes Magazine and Author of The Billion Dollar Bet, the story or John Johnson's rise to a billionaire. Brett and I attended Hampton University together and it was Brett that gave me the inspiration to finally complete this work. I commend his ability as a writer and journalist, he is one of the best in the business and his book the Billion Dollar Bet is an outstanding look at how far one can go, if they only seek to be. Brett Pulley, my friend and college mate has definitely been a great inspiration to me, in my attempt to keep on growing.

Governor Roy Barnes. For four years I truly will remember how this man made education the number one priority of his administration. He provided the leadership to successfully craft and pass the most comprehensive and ambitious education reform in the history of Georgia. As a result of his commitment my grandson and countless others will benefit from the educational opportunities which Georgia has in place. Governor Barnes also pushed for the tax and health care reform, the three major areas the people of Georgia so desperately needed during his administration. A soft spoken man with a heavy conviction to serve all the people, now that's what leadership is all about.

Denzel Washington. In college I majored in Speech and Drama, and minored in Communications, so theatre, movies and the media have always been apart of my inspiration as well as motivation. I have watched actors grow and evolve and there are so many great ones out there. But then there's Denzel Washington. You can tell he's a God fearing man by his presence alone. God has truly touched this great actor, and I look up to him as a truly victorious example of what God can and what God will do. My wife Daphine can attest that we do not miss any of Denzel's movies. Denzel Washington, I salute you!

Rev. Christopher Ervin and his wife Daphine reside in Atlanta Georgia. Rev. Ervin has and continues to pen hundreds of inspiring poems lifting the name of Jesus Christ. He is a Senior Associate Minister at Lindsay Street Baptist Church in Atlanta, Georgia. His two greatest loves are Preaching the Gospel, and writing inspirational poetry, lifting the name of Jesus Christ everywhere he goes. His future plans include turning his poems to song, along with the creation of Inspirational Movies and video documentary presentations aimed at the continued building and education for those interested in growing in their walk with God. He enjoys reading his poetry, speaking and preaching at revivals, seminars, and special events to audiences of all ages, races, genders and nationalities. He prides himself as always being available for the people of God.

Uplifting…
Inspiring…
Powerful…
Poems for the Believer!

A collection of poems,
formed to take you
higher!

Ego's or Eagles

Egos have made,
Small men great.
Egos are the guides,
To our programmed fate.
Through the ditches and jungles,
The ups and downs.
Through the mountains and trees,
Our egos must fly,
For if they lie in their nest,
They will surely die.
Yes, it is true,
Egos must fly.

I Will Plant My Feet In The Soil

I will plant my feet in the soil,
And grow like a tree.
Rising to great heights,
My Master and me.
In my arms there will be power,
My hair,
Leafs of the free.
I shall grow each day and hour,
My Master and me.
I shall never harm a soul,
I shall always live in peace,
And never stop my growing,
Until my life doth cease.
And when I die,
I shall leave my root,
For life is the gift,
The gift of God's fruit.
And so shall the seed,
Of this great loved fruit,
Return to the soil,
To become a new root.
And I shall return again and again,
And always grow,
Again and again,
I shall always win.
For I am as the seed and the tree,
In God's great land.

The Dare Devils

The dare devils,
They know who they are.
Defying death to become a star.
They live their lives,
In question each day.
Chancing that nature,
Won't take them away.
The dare devils,
Displaying feats,
Ever so great.
The dare devils,
Do they question their fate?
The dare devils are here today,
And some of their followers,
Say they're here to stay,
Defying new challenges,
In a grand new way!
And from these great new challenges,
They shall never stray.
The dare devils,
For them I pray.

If People Could See

Never before has there been a people so free,
Unaware of the privileges,
They know should be.

Oh, what a world if this people could see.
Their conditions have surpassed,
All so many,
While in upward mobility,
They have suffered passed plenty.

The unity died when a man paid the cost,
While seeking to be free,
His life he lost.
Then somehow the unity died,
Then some how so died the pride.

Oh, what a world if this people could see.
They would look in the past,
Past all the pain,
Look through the dry spells,
And look for the rain.

They would look for that person,
They once had lost.
They would look for the reason,
They're paying the cost.

They would look at the problems,
They couldn't foresee.
Look in the past,
And find the key.

They'd look for love,
And look for peace.
They'd look for the day,
When war would cease.

They'd look to God,
And pray for help,
And they'd look to action,
To be their rep.

Oh, what a world if this people could see.

The New Generation

The new generation to me seems asleep,
Lost from their shepherd,
Poor, poor sheep.

Lost in a land with thousands of roads,
Lost in a world with millions of codes

The new generation has a lot to learn,
Though it seems they only listen,
When the fires start to burn.

What they need is a map,
To plot their course.
For with belief in themselves,
They're a solid force.

With the map and the strength,
They just might proceed.
And only then,
If they all can read,
The new generation,
Just might succeed!

The Power of Thought

The power of thought,
Is a powerful sphere,
It stands alone.
And when motivated,
Knows no fear.

As it journeys on its own,
In its flights to new eras,
It's discovering hidden caves,
And beneath them many terrors.

The power of thought
Can create would peace.
Or end all of life,
Yes, a world deceased.

This power of thought,
Which created our wealth,
Seems to have suddenly lost,
Its nourished health.

Depressions are heavy,
Conditions are poor,
And as deficits continue,
In an endless score,
Has the power of thought,
Closed it's door?

Man's Need

What does man need,
In these times so unfair?
While jobs are in decline,
And workers in a scare.

Production slowing down,
And products in despair.
What does man need,
In these times so unfair?

Budget deficits at an all time high,
While our women and children,
Do nothing but cry.
And when hit with fatal disease,
We eye each other,
Why?

Our preachers say,
We need to look to the Lord.
While politicians preach,
The power of Ford.

Do politicians have the answers,
Religion or we?
The answer my friends,
Can set us free.

Mankind simply needs to wake up,
And see!
Find peace in God,
Which giveth strength.
Find peace in He,
And discover true length.

Put your hand in the Father's,
And you'll find a true friend.
And soon you will find,
That your troubles will all end.
What does man need in these times so unfair?
Simply love,
With a powerful prayer.

I Had a Dream Last Night

I had a dream last night
It would be all right.
I had a dream last night,
And was it out of sight!

A dream of peace and love throughout the land.
A dream where wars throughout the world,
Had all been banned.

Where men and women lived in love,
And all the whole world,
Knew of God above.

Boy, did I have a dream last night!

The president and politicians were always fair,
And men who thought of crimes?
They wouldn't even dare.

Cities were large,
And everyone employed.
And with other men's women,
No one toyed.

Love throughout a land,
Once filled with hate and disease.
Peace in the land,
Where no one would freeze.

God in action each and every day.
People lived in harmony,
And everyone would pray.

Life never ending,
Only rescinding.
Songs never dying,
Children never crying,
And good always defying.

Boy, did I have a dream last night.

Homes for everyone,
And no one left out.
Peace everywhere,
As children ran about.

Drugs disappeared,
And everywhere they cheered!
It seemed like not a dream,
But a thought well planned.

Boy, did I have a dream last night.

Times of Tribulation

Times of Tribulation are in the air,
People are feeling it everywhere.
Poison in the water,
Poison in the air,
It seems like life itself,
Isn't even fair.

Anger steadily showing
Armies steadily growing,
And we constantly read in the papers,
Of crashes by a Boeing.

People starving and children crying,
Men and women with diseases dying.
Times of tribulations are suddenly here.

Neighboring countries always fighting.
The constant sound of lightning.
And it seems somehow frightening,
How tribulations reappear.

The Bible speaks of revelations,
Where as men speak of realizations,
And while the world is filled with a host of frustrations,
Now's the time of tribulation.

I Shall Give and Follow

I shall give to my Lord,
My all and all,
And then I shall wait,
To hear His call.
If I give all I've got,
I can never fail.
For when I build with my Father,
My ship is sure to sail.
My strength is great,
I am not weak,
As I walk with the Lord,
I walk at my peak,
I am built of stone,
No evil can break,
I shall never be broken,
My Lord, I shall never forsake.
He has given me hope,
To bear each hour.
He has given me strength,
Given me power.
As I walk in His steps,
Others shall follow.
His powers are strong.
His waters not shallow.
And never has his love for mankind,
Ever been hollow.
To my Lord, my God,
I shall give and follow.

To See Men Compete

To see men compete is to witness great challenge,
Mind and body over matter,
Competition without chatter.

The mind and the body must claim full control,
For when a man competes,
It is his greatest role.

Each blow must be direct,
Each counter without fear,
For winning it seems,
Is the only care.

And then when its over,
One stands alone,
Until the next contest,
A trophy gains a home.

But that to may change,
By the end of the next feat.
Oh, what joy,
To see men compete.

As The Struggle Goes On

As the struggle goes on to find world peace,
Our ghettoes live in a hell, which will never cease.
Babies crying all through the night,
Junkies shooting up left and right.

And if you're looking for a friend,
You'd better stay in the light.
As inflation reaches an all time high,
Politicians keep saying, "Keep your heads to the sky",

But how when inflation never seems to die?
Rats living good at an all time high,
Roaches and junkies, that think they can fly.
And not a person in the ghetto without an alibi.

Some are living good, with their big bad rides,
Living in homes washed down by the tides.
Trying to find a job, where they're laying people off.
Trying to find a meal just to stay aloft.

When it's 6 a.m. in the city where I live,
The struggle just begins and from their it never gives.
As the struggle goes on,
So will time.
And that my friend is a very poor rhyme,
But the struggle goes on,
And that's a very good sign.
Because the struggle goes on.

The Challenge

Here is a challenge,
To you I do not know.
Here is a challenge,
For you to grow.

I dare you to dream,
Of world wide peace.
I dare you to pray,
That poverty cease.

I dare you to lead men,
In these theories of love,
Knowing that all answers,
Come from above.

And knowing in that mission,
It is earth you must lead,
I dare you to fight,
And not retreat.

I challenge you to suffer,
All you men of great wealth.
And seek to end the millions,
Of our children's deaths.

I challenge you to fight,
Honest and fare.
I challenge you to seek,
That each get their share.
I challenge you to this,
My prayer.

Success

Success is God,
In the hearts of men.
Success is protection,
From the wages of sin.

Success is God in action,
In a world with problems too many.
Success is when people are free,
No strings attached to any.

Success is simply being there,
Where ever you want to be.
Success is going everywhere,
See what you want to see.

Success is God in action,
For you and for me.

The Power of Prayer

The power of prayer,
Is showing everywhere.
Throughout the whole world.
It's as plain as the air.

Thanks to all Christians which stand by their faith.
It is because of their prayers, our world is still safe.
Leaders keep on coming, and the lost stop their stumbling.
As the number of Christians continue to grow,
The power of prayer will ultimately show,
There's no power in the world,
As great as the one we know.

Peace and love to those who believe in prayer,
Peace and love to their loved ones, everywhere.
It is in prayer that we find answers to our problems so many.
And it is in prayer that we find strength for situations,
Too unfriendly.

Prayer is a gift,
The good Lord has given us,
Prayer is the light for the weak, blind and frivolous.
The power of prayer will continue to show.

That truly God is able,
And helps all Christians grow.
The power of prayer,
Is a power all should know.

Just A Little Nip and Tuck

Just a little nip and tuck,
And everything will change.
Just a little here and there.
Your face they'll rearrange.

Just a little off, on the left and the right.
The world will see a difference,
just like day and just like night!

You'll pay a high cost,
For this marvelous need.
The Doctors will truly love you,
You buy their knits and their tweeds.

Just a little nip and tuck,
You'll gain a brand new high.
But don't be fooled my friend,
In a year look again,
It's time again to buy!

God In Action Inc.

God's in action,
Night and day.
All around the world,
In every kind of way.

God has been there throughout the wars,
All over the world.
God is in the cores and hearts,
Of men and women,
Boys and girls.

God is in action,
Even in space,
As men continue to explore,
Their simple disgrace,
This vast and open Place.

God is in action,
When leaders take stands.
God is in action, When people hold hands.

When the hurricanes,
Floods and earthquakes heighten,
It will be God in action,
So Christians, don't be frightened.

Throughout this world of chaos,
God will continue to show,
For God in action,
Is older than we know.

Through politics, weather, disease and wars,
It is God that watches over us, even the whore's.

God is in action,
And His actions are growing stronger.
As Christians continue to grow,
Satan shall live no longer.

One day God in Action,
Will be an Institution,
Where the troubled and the lost,
Shall escape their confusions.

My Lord and I

The time is now and place is here,
I shall let go my feelings,
And let go my fear.

I was born of parents,
Strong believers in God.
They believe in the Ten Commandments,
And in the power of the Lord's rod.

They gave to their son
as they gave to their daughters,
Knowing not how they'd survive high waters.
They taught us of love and taught us of God.
They taught us of peace and of nothing odd.

They provided us with a home,
which gave us a brand new high,
They gave us all we ever needed, my sister's and I.
I thank the Lord for giving them to me,
I thank the Lord for setting me free.
To walk this land, living within God's laws.

I've found a lot, but not enough.
I've learned a lot, one thing be tough.

My love of family has always been strong,
My love of people, has lasted me long.
I shall always thank God above.

He has given me life and given me love.
He has shown me how to love and not hate.
He has taught me how to let, my pains dissipate.
He has given me a reason to sing and shout!
Given me strength, to live without doubt.

He has given me strength in times of pain.
He has pulled me out, of the endless rain.
The Lord has shown me how to live, in a world full of hate,
Shown me the truth the true Christians fate.

Somehow I know, my Father will never leave me alone,
For I pray day and night, to the glory of His throne.
He has given me strength to bare all pain,
Given me shelter from the endless rain.

Given me a home, Where I may lay down,
He walks with me wherever I go,
He has been with me, wherever I show.

And there is one thing, that I know for sure,
I shall love Him always, and my love shall be pure .
He has given me more, than any could ever,
He has given me life, and regret it I'll never.

The Lord has done for me, what no others could do,
He has given me family, and problems so few.
I cannot but wonder why the Lord, has done this for me,
But He has given me something,
In that, He's given me He.

Thank God For
The Good People In The World

Thank God for the good people in the world.
Their light shines so brightly,
For men and women,
Boys and girls.

They give to the world all of themselves,
Leaving hate and greed, where they belong,
On the shelves.

There motto is simple,
All for one and one for all.
For without that one thought,
The world would fall.

They live each day,
Each moment and hour,
In hopes that the world,
Would learn of God's power.

Their light shines so brightly,
Not just in the day, but also nightly.
And they constantly pray,
To God the Father Almighty.

They give to the poor,
And care for the needy.
They despise all evil.
As well as the greedy.

Thank God for the good people in the world,
For through their actions we learn,
To live in peace and love,
And give graciously each day,
To pray to our Father in heaven,
Not to let us go astray.

Thank God for the good people in this world.
They make me want to shout!
Praising the Father in Heaven,
For sending us good people,
Those we could never doubt.

We're All In This Together

We're all in this together,
You can't run and you can't hide,
And by certain rules we all must abide.

We're all in this together,
You and I,
Whether we laugh,
Or whether we cry,

It's for certain one day,
We all must die.
We all must fight,
For what we feel is right.
We all have pains,
And sometimes sleep in fright.

We all do fear,
The things we do not know.
We all do cheer,
When in happiness we glow.

We're all in this together,
This thing which we call life.
And either we all fight together,
Or continue to live in strife.

We're all in this together,
And you say, when will it end?
When life is no more,
And all cease to be.
When the wind stops blowing.
And there is no disease.

When there is no more water,
And the sun doesn't shine.
When the world has come to an end.
And there's no such thing as time.

Only then will it by ended,
This life we've come to know,
The time we finally separate,
The end of the show.

So remember dear friends.
Where ever in life you go,
We're all in this together,
Till when?
*   Only God knows.*

A Simple Explanation

The year 2004.
The conditions of times,
Very, very poor.

The world in depression,
People going insane.
Some for money and power,
Others for fame.

The cause of this atmosphere is self-evident,
And beyond a shadow of a doubt, the same cause,
That effected our forefathers and those before them.
Man's need to be something he could never be.
God is omnipotent, omniscient and omnipresent,
The creator and maker of all things,
Man felt the need to do the same,
Feeling that he,
Was a supreme being.

So man began to build great empires,
And cities of great wealth.
Armies of great strength,
And the science of good health.

And soon the world began to grow and grow,
And all the time technology would show,
That man could go far, if he seeked to know.

And so man did seek,
Climbing mountains ever so high.
Studying the oceans and the forest,
Knowledge would always be his cry.
And for centuries to come,
Mankind would always seek,
To know what's in the earth,
Above it and beneath.

And still mankind seeks to know,
More than any other.
To grow to great heights,
No mater what the cost to his brothers.
Heaven these men shall never see,
For they dream of only,
How great they can be.

The Beast

There is a beast in this world,
Which has no face.
And as it lingers in various bodies,
It is mankind's disgrace.

It is a devil in disguise
That punishes the unwise.
Seeking crime and terror,
For the world's demise.

The beasts I speak of,
Could be so called friends and neighbors,
Pretending to stand by your side,
Throughout your pains and labors.

Yes, it is true,
This beast has no face.
And it dwells in the minds,
Of the whole human race.

In your minds and mine,
It seeks a permanent home.
A place to plan its evil,
And cause the world to moan.

It is this beast we must fight,
And fight without fear.
For the beast is mighty clever,
And always near.

Pray to God,
For the beast to leave you alone.
And the beast will surely leave you,
Through the power of his throne.

When God Cries

When God cries,
God cries for the world.
All the men and women,
All the boys and girls,
He cries for the rich,
As well as the poor,
God cries because he loves us,
And nothing more.

God cries for all our sins,
But do we ever question why?
God's heart is so strong,
That none shall he deny.

For God so love the world,
He gave His only Begotten Son,
Not to prove a thing,
For all battles God has won.

And yet God still gives,
In life, love and labors.
God still watches over us,
You, I and our neighbors.

When God cries,
It is the world which is suffering,
For we know not the greatness,
Of His tender and warm loving.

But when God stops crying,
The world will surely know,
As the change in the weather,
Continues to show.

And the day shall come,
When the world shall see,
The anger of God,
And the powers that be.

And God shall cry no more,
For all will of had their chance.
Pain shall rule the world,
And the Godly shall sing and dance.

That is the time,
When God shall cry no more,
When sinners throughout the world,
Shall feel His inner core.
Christians be ready,
For we know not the date,
When God's love and compassion,
Dissipates.
And God shall cry,
                              No more.

Passing On

It's a mysterious thing,
How in life we pass on.
Suddenly we're here,
And suddenly we're gone.

Time can be funny,
Time can be quick,
Just as a drink,
Sometimes thin,
Sometimes thick.

And as we pass on,
In this life we live.
How much do we learn,
And how much do we give?

At times I look at nature,
And then I look to the sky.
I look to the trees,
As the wind passes by.

It seems I hear them cry.
Then I look to the stars,
So high in the sky.

And I think of God's great people,
Who have lived and died.
Now they watch over us,
And hear our every cry,
For they are the angels,
Those stars in the sky.

Some of those stars,
Have passed on through grace.
A gift which is truly won.
Others have passed through love,
Which comes from the Father's Son.

Those which did not pass,
Are those which had never begun.
To understand that in life,
Within the Father we must be One.
So if you're true to the Lord,
And true to His Son,
Never fear in this life,
Passing on.

A Time In Life

There comes a time in life,
When we come to the Lord.
A time in life,
When we live by the sword.

A time when the Father,
Gives us peace.
A time when pain and war,
Suddenly cease.

When children stop crying,
The good stop dying,
And the word of God, undenying.

A time in life,
When peace shall reign.
And thunder and lightning,
Resemble our pain.

A time of death,
As evil ones lose their health.
When the sun shall not rise,
And who shall know the answers?
Only the wise.

Read the words contained in the Bible,
For without that knowledge,
We are all held liable.

For there shall come a time in life,
We shall all close our eyes,
Too late for forgiveness,
Of sins and lies.

When life is no more,
And our Father in Heaven,
Shall record our score.
Just remember one thing,
Win or lose,
There comes a time in life,
For all to choose.

The Rebels Are Coming

The rebels are coming,
And as though sent from a star.
They're changing the world,
But for the better by far.

The rebels are coming,
And they shall succeed.
With strong testimonies,
Of how this world has made us bleed.

Their awakening this world,
To how it can be.
Bringing the message of the Lord,
Which is the power of the free.

Telling of the innocent who've died,
Of the countries with no pride.
And Presidents who've all lied.

Freeing the world of the blunders so frequent,
The rebels are coming!
And not delinquent.

Who are these rebels?
They you can't see,
For they are the powers,
Within you and me.

A power so strong,
A rebel so free.
Rebels of peace,
With love as their decree.

And who is the enemy,
That these rebels must fight?
Those negative ways of the world,
Which keeps us from the light.
For the people of this world,
Like you and me.
The rebels fight,
With a will to be free.

A Thanksgivings Day Prayer

Now is the time for thanks and giving,
Now is the time of Godly living.
Thanks for the food you've placed at our tables,
And thank you for our strength,
for it truly makes us able.
Thank you for this life,
In which happiness is full.
Thank you for our health,
And winter clothes of wool.
Thank you Lord,
For simply giving us strength,
The ability to love,
And to give our tenth.
Help us to share our feelings for you.
Help others to see and others to view,
That those who walk with thee,
Shall never be few.
We ask that you watch over,
The sick and the needy.
Give strength and hope,
To those who are greedy.
Help us to see,
Thou's ever shining light.
Through our troubles and pains,
In the days and night.
Feel our hearts and souls with desire,
Take us Father,
Please take us higher!
Now is the time to give Thanksgiving,
Because thou hast blessed us,
With Christian ways of living.
                    Amen.

All The People, Where Did They Go!

All the people,
Where did they go?
Our country in flames,
And how?
No one knows.

All the people,
They said they would fight!
Yet here I stand alone,
At the edge of the night.

All the people,
Where did they go?
They said when it was time,
They'd surely show,
And fight for the things,
That would help us to grow.
Will someone please tell me,
Where'd all the people go?

King, A Master Mind

I know of a man,
Who once spoke of peace,
Until his life,
Came to a cease.

Martin Luther King,
Was great in his time.
He shall always be remembered,
As a superior mind.

He spoke of peace and love,
Throughout all nations.
He spoke of God above,
And the essence of revelations.

He gave to men and women,
A new way of thinking.
How the world could one day be,
Without war and bombs shrieking.

He spoke of being great,
And just what it would take.
Serving the Lord,
In a world unawake.

He served his country,
Without fear of dying.
He served the world,
Without ever lying.

And now the world has changed,
To a finer way of living.
Now men and women,
Know the purpose of giving.

He spoke of great leaders,
And all that they sought.
To be looked upon by people,
As great people ought.

And now he has gone,
But his spirit still survives,
In the hearts of men and women,
In all of our lives.

Martin Luther King,
Was a great, great man.
For he prayed to our Father in Heaven,
For the master plan.

Dr. King was God in action,
For God worked through his life.
Giving to the world,
A great need to entice.

Now I know the meaning,
Of being a leader.
Of being great and giving,
Not just a senseless needer.

To serve the Lord is to serve all mankind,
And that is the greatness,
That all true leaders find.
Martin Luther King,
A master mind.

What's Happening To Our People?

What's happening to our people,
In these times so unsure,
While wars are in the making,
And so called Christians so impure?

The poisoning of our foods,
And the threatening of our lives.
It seems we no longer care,
Yet in our fears we all grow hives.

What's happening to our people,
In this land once so free?
Where men and women,
Boys and girls,
Can decide what they want to be?

Our own people,
Threatening each other!
Do they realize,
They threaten their own sisters and brothers?

Is Revelations suddenly here?
If so, my friends,
We should all be in fear.
For millions will die,
And all shall cry.

It will be too late for wondering,
What, if and why?
What's happening to our people?

Wake up and see!

Traveling On The Main Course

There's a course in life,
Which will take you,
Wherever you want to go.
It may be sometimes bumpy,
But the signs will let you know.
The course may be short,
Though it's mostly always long.
So remember to take the right one,
For it doesn't pay to take the wrong.
And if through your many travels,
You find the road to success.
Just remember one thing,
In your life dream quests,
When choosing a path,
Or course which you will travel,
Watch for curves and downgrades,
And roads sometimes narrow.
Never close your eyes,
For the course may sometimes change.
Look out for oncoming traffic,
Or your life will be rearranged.
And remember when you choose your course,
To drive straight and steady,
With all of your power and all of your force,
To show that you are ready.
Don't forget to take God with you,
And you'll know the true meaning of success,
Traveling on the main course,
Of life's never ending quests.

Never Run Away

Never run away,
For it doesn't help a thing.
Never run away,
For that's a song which cowards sing.

Never be afraid,
To turn and fight,
Never run away,
Whether day or night.

Remember to stand steady,
And give all you've got.
Never run away,
Or in this life with fear you'll rot.

Stand tall and face your enemies,
And pray to God for power.
And you shall live your life in serenity,
Each day, each night, and hour.

Never run away,
For you'll let down the human race.
Think of the boys and girls,
The people you'll disgrace.

No one likes a coward,
So never run away.
Stick to your dreams and hopes,
And from them never stray.
One more thing to remember,
Don't forget to pray.

The Circus

Some say the circus is coming,
I say it's already here,
So should we sing in happiness,
Or live in fear?

The circus which I speak of,
Is the circus some call life.
Sometimes filled with so much happiness,
Other times with strife.

Where politicians like clowns
Can be so unfunny,
And the cost of water,
Is the same as honey.

Men and women never trusting each other,
Women loving women,
And men in love with their brothers.
Where inflation seems to fly,
The number of poor continue to grow,
At a new record high.
And for the cause of war?
There's no alibi.

Some say the circus is coming,
I say it's already here.
There is no charge for admission,
Just step in the ring if you dare.
Remember one thing,
And that's never look down,
And I'm sure you'll find,
That the circus is in town.

The Race

The race was long,
But I kept my stride.
I was surely in pain,
And that I couldn't hide.

I gave it my all,
Though breathing got harder,
I gave it my all,
And kept going further.

Suddenly a pain struck me in my chest.
But I kept on running,
And I didn't think of rest.

Soon I saw my goal,
Which kept me keeping on,
I wouldn't stop running,
Until the race was won.

Then came the light,
Still as I was running.
Suddenly I stopped,
And thought myself cunning!

I had run till the dawn.

The Mansion

There is a place I know of,
That sits all so high.
This place which I speak of,
Is a mansion in the sky.

This mansion is full,
Of pride and glory,
So on with this,
Godly story.

I know of a mansion,
Built of stone,
And those which occupied it's rooms,
Would never be alone.

It sat high on a mountain,
Surrounded by clouds in the sky.
No evil could penetrate,
Its perilous high.

This mansion which I speak of,
I saw in my sleep,
While in slumber I saw Jesus Christ,
I suddenly began to weep.

In this mansion were many rooms,
And they never seemed to end.
A place for all of God's righteous people,
Which glowed with many a friend.

I also saw that they moaned and cried,
They moaned for the sheep,
That would simply live and die.
For those lost sheep,
Would never see,
This mansion also high.

When I awoke,
I went straight to my knees,
Praying to my Father,
To hear my plea.

Of the sin in this world,
Please set me free!
Now I pray,
Night and day.
That I'll one day occupy,
A room in God's mansion,

And from it never stray.

Lead Us

Father lead us,
From our enemy,
And of sin and hatred,
Please set us free.

Strengthen us Father,
Night and day,
Lead us father,
All the way.

You've brought us from,
Our mothers' wombs.
Freed your son,
From a stone covered tomb.
Please lead us Father,
Through these lifeless rooms.

Lead us Father,
Through our tribulas lives,
Lead us Father,
Both husbands and wives.
Lead our children,
As you lead us,
Lead us Father,
For it is you we trust.

How Far Can I Go?

How far can I go?
Watch me my friend,
And you soon shall know.

What mountains can I climb,
What valleys can I reach?
What strength have I now?
Just listen to me preach.

I can climb the highest mountain,
Swim the seven seas.
For the Lord is in my heart,
And it is He I seek to please.

I can run a thousand miles,
conquer the greatest kings,
I can fly like a dove,
With golden wings.

I can go anywhere,
Do anything.
For the power of my Lord,
Is the power of the Supreme.

How far can I go?
Ask those who serve the Lord,
I'm sure they'll let you know.

Inspiration

Inspiration is something
Which we gain through life,
After traveling down the road
Of love and strife.

Great men are inspired to act by God,
So they live their lives in peace,
Which some see as odd.

They give to the world,
All in their hearts.
Praying that through love
The world will gain a new art.

Christians are inspired
By the greatness of their faith
And that is the reason we give
Tenths and not eighths.

I have been inspired,
To write this short book,
In hopes that in life,
The world would look.
And see what I see,
Christ waiting at the brook..

God has inspired me,
How about you?
Remember when inspired,
Your weaknesses are few.

Study God's Word

Study God's word,
And from it you shall grow.
And all in the world will surely know.
It will show in the way you live,
And your life will surely glow.

Study to show thyself,
Approved unto God.
Study to show that in your life,
Nothing is odd.

Study to gain power for life,
Study to gain freedom from strife.
Study to maintain a positive outlook in life.
Study to overcome evil and vice.
Study so that through you,
Others can learn.

Study God's word,
And leave evil ones to burn.
Study for the children,
So they may grow in your ways.
Study my friend,
To lengthen your days.

Study to understand,
The way the world must be.
Study to comprehend,
What others can't see.
The power of God's love,
A love so free.

Horizons Are Coming

Horizons are coming,
A day of relief!
Horizons are coming,
No more grief.

Horizons are coming,
When Christ returns.
Horizons are coming,
As sure as the world does turn.

Christians will cheer!
It will be all so clear,
That horizons are coming,
And there is nothing to fear.
Yes, horizons are coming,
Christ so dear.

What Shall I Call Him?

What shall I call Him, Father or God?
What shall I call Him,
In this life so odd?

Shall I call Him Jehovah, Master or Lord?
Or shall I call Him,
The wonderful King and Messiah,
Which rules without a sword?

Whatever I call him,
The name means the same.
For there is only one ruler,
None surpass His fame.

There is only one ruler,
Which truly stands alone.
Only one ruler,
There can be no other clones.

Whether you call Him,
God, Lord, Jehovah, or Messiah,
Whether you call Him,
King or Father,
You are no liar.
For He is all and everything,
For He is our Father, Lover and King.

I Called

I called for you,
And you did not answer.
I called for you,
Though you acted as,
A whorish dancer.
I called for you,
But you did not hear.
I called for you,
But I, you did not fear.
I called for you,
While you worshipped false masters.
I called for you,
Both before and after.
You knew of my powers,
And you knew my name.
You knew of my son,
Who else could I blame?
You've seen my powers,
And love in action.
You knew the wages of sin,
Yet it was still your attraction.
I called for you,
And spoke your name.
Giving you my blessings,
I saved you from the flames.
I gave my only Son,
So that you would not suffer.
I gave you all of my love,
As could no other.
I called for you,
Now it's your turn.

Why Am I Different?

Why am I different,
It seems the world wants to know.
Why am I different,
And seem to constantly grow?

Why do I walk in love each day,
Though anger and evil always come my way?
Why do I seek to grow each day and hour,
Searching for the strength and light of God's power?

Why do I think and act as I do?
If you read the scriptures,
You'd change too!

Lost

I was lost among a crowd,
Which knew not right from wrong.
Lost among a crowd,
Not knowing what I had become.

I was lost in a life,
Not knowing which way to go.
Lost in a world,
In which nothing had I to show.

I was lost in thought,
Not knowing what I had sought.
Not thinking of the days passing by,
Nor of the pain which I'd be taught.

I was lost until I found God,
Which carried me through life.
Throughout times of tribulations,
Endless troubles and times of strife.

Then I was given a chance,
Through the grace of God the Father.
Then I was given a chance,
To grow and travel further.
And I was lost no more.

Found

No longer am I lost,
Thanks to the grace of God.
No longer am I lost,
Nor living a life so odd.
No longer shall I wonder,
Where in life did I go wrong?
For now I've heard the voice,
Which sings the greatest song.
No longer shall I question,
Where in life am I to go?
No longer shall I seek,
The things which won't help me to grow.
No longer shall I cry,
And ask the Father why,
The troubles in the world,
Never seem to die?
No longer shall I fear,
The fact that one day I must die.
No longer shall I fear,
The things which cause me to sigh.
No longer shall I fight,
The power I feel within.
For now I give to Christ,
My love which has no end.
No longer shall I question,
The direction in which my father sends me.
And no longer shall I live,
A life of sinful envy.
For now, I am found.

Here I Sit Alone

Here I sit all alone,
No one knows my troubles,
Nor the location of my home.
No one knows I'm angered,
No one knows my fears,
Yet here I sit alone,
Holding in my tears.
No one sees me crying,
No one sees me sighing,
No one knows my pain,
Or of the fact that I am dying.
Here I sit alone,
While others sit in company.
Here I sit alone,
Watching the world in all its tyranny.
While others sit, laugh and talk,
I sit and stalk,
Thinking of my fears,
And the life in which I walk.
Here I sit alone,
Praying to my Lord.
Here I sit alone,
I and the Father, on one accord.
Here I sit alone,
Wondering of my burden's length,
Here I sit alone,
Praying for my lord's great strength.
Yes, here I sit alone,
But soon, I too will have company,
When Christ my Lord returns,
For all the world to see.

Come Back, My People

Come back my people,
You've been gone for so long.
Come back my people,
And praise Christ the Lord,
With love and new songs.
Come back and repent.
Come back my people,
And I shall renew thine strength!
Come back my people,
And with my love, I shall bless thee.
Come back my people,
And through your light which shines so brightly,
The world shall truly see.
The Lord is forgiving.
The Lord is Loving.
And the Lord shall bless,
All of those returning.
You left me to praise,
False God's and idols.
Yet you return to me,
When your lives become trifle.
Come back my people,
And I shall set thee free,
And of thine enemies in this world,
None shall there be.
Come back my people,
And through my eyes,
You shall see!

Which Way Do I Go?

Which way do I go,
And which road should I travel?
What should I do,
As life's puzzles unravel?
Which way do I go?
Which things should I know?
Which things should I learn,
Which could help my life to grow?
Which prayer should I use,
Which scriptures should I choose?
Which passages should I read?
Lord please help me, I'm confused.
The thoughts which are in my heart,
Confuse me all too much,
For there are so many roads to travel,
Within my manly clutch.
Which way do I go,
When my troubles are so great?
Which way do I go,
And to whom shall I relate?
Which things should I think?
Which things should I know?
Which way should I act?
How should my heart's thoughts flow?
Father please guide me,
The way thou would have me to go.

The Lesson

There is a lesson in life,
For all the world to learn.
Though it seems we only listen,
When the fires start to burn.
Though at times our lessons differ,
You must never in life forget,
The lessons we all learn,
Are taught by the greatest giver.
There are lessons of peace,
And lessons of love,
Which can only come,
From Christ above.
Those who do not listen,
Are those who will truly learn,
When Christ the Lord returns,
To the people of His concern.
Pray that all be ready,
Study and grow in God's light.
And pray that all be strong enough,
To battle Satan's might.
If you have not studied,
Remember it's never too late,
For forgiveness from the Lord,
Is nothing to debate.
Pray that the Scriptures will show you,
The lessons all should learn.
That within God the Father,
We all must be one.

I Have a Mission

I have a mission,
And a job to fulfill.
I have a mission,
And do it I will.

I promised the Lord,
I would serve His name.
Giving to Christ,
All the fame.

I have a mission,
To bring the lost to Christ.
I have a mission,
That I must do while there's still light.

I cannot stop,
For the days pass too quickly.
I cannot stop,
For the world still grows sickly.

I have a mission,
To make sure all know of the Lord,
I have a mission,
And with my Father in Heaven,
I'm on one accord.

I have a mission
To fight sin and evil.
I have a mission,
And there can be no retrieval.
I have a mission,
What about you?

Today

Today may be one of the greatest days of your life.
For it's another day of living,
Which God has given us through Christ.
A day which we should all be thankful for,
That God has opened our eyes,
To a new and more beautiful day,
To see the sun rise.

Each night before I sleep,
I pray to my Father in Heaven,
Please allow me to awake the next morning,
At the dawning hour of seven.

Today we should be thankful,
For everything in life.
Today we should be thankful,
For the life of Jesus Christ.

For Christ did die on Calvary one day,
And Christ did give His life,
Which washed our sins away.
Christ did truly lead the way,
To a new and more beautiful,
Today.

When Things Aren't Going Your Way

When there are times of troubles,
And it seems they never end.
When there are times of need,
And you can't seem to find a friend.

When there are times you're down,
And don't seem to think clear.
When there are times of frowns,
And answers don't seem near.

That's the time to pray,
To the Lord who's always there.
When things don't seem to fit,
Nothing seems to click,
And it seems you can't even,
Get in the first lick.

That's the time my friend,
You really need to pray.
And remember in this life,
That nothing can last forever,
Remember that one fact,
And regret it you'll never.

And if by chance,
You allow Christ, to enter into you life,
You'll find new ways to deal,
With your pains and strife's.

Still one other thing,
That you should learn.
those who play with fire,
Are sure to gain a burn.

Stick with God,
And you can always say,
In times of troubles,
When things aren't going your way,
At least I'm not the fool,
Which knows not how to pray.

Seek, Ask and Pray

Seek, ask and pray,
That the world will find a way,
To surpass the sin and evilness,
We battle day to day.

Seek and you will find,
All that is mine.
Seek and you shall find,
His lovingness so kind.

Seek and find the answers,
Which all men question in life.
Seek to end the thousands,
Of lives never ending strife's.

Seek the Father to carry you,
to places you could not go.
Seek God the Father,
And in His love, your life will grow.

Seek and ye shall know.
Seek, ask and pray,
And as sure as the Lord saved Israel,
He will surely come your way.

Ask and it will be given,
But truly you must believe.
Ask and it will be given,
For divine power you shall receive.

Ask the Father for cures,
For problems and disease.
Ask the Father for strength,
That of evil you aren't deceived
Pray to God the Father,
And His loving son.
Pray that one bright day,
We shall overcome.

Pray that you will learn,
The power of His love.
Pray for the sinners and sickly in this world,
Pray to God above.

Don't be like the heathens,
Which thank they have all in life.
For the riches of this world,
Are the causes of our strife's.

Pray that you will find,
That after life you have a friend.
Pray that through this life,
All God's lessons you will have learned.

Pray to God the Father,
That forgiveness you have earned.
Pray that God's in action,
And your life will take a turn.
Seek, ask and pray!

People of the World

People of the world,
Come from many places.
Thousands of different cities,
And so many different races.
Some are shades of white,
Some are shades of brown.
Some are living high,
And some are living down.
Some speak several languages,
Some speak only one.
Some have strong beliefs,
And some have none.
People of the world,
All have something in common.
Whether the need to simply live in peace,
Or a life quiet and solemn.
All seek to know,
The things which will help them to grow.
All seek to find,
The freedom to rule their own minds.
People of the world,
All need to know of Christ,
People of the world,
All need Christ in their lives.
For no one has the power,
To change their color or nature,
Yet all need the power,
Which can come only from the Savior.
People of the world,
All need Christ.

A Purpose in Life

We all inevitably have a purpose in life
Whether to live simple and normal lives,
Or to serve this world, so full of strife's.
Our purposes may to us
Yet be unknown.
But within this life we all live,
They shall one day be shown.
Some people have a purpose to lead.
Others to follow,
Some to seek power,
While others simply seek,
To remain in the shadows.
Some have a purpose to give life,
To the leaders of tomorrow.
While others have a purpose,
To bring this world sorrow.
All shall come to know,
Whether early or late in life,
All people have a purpose.
And though it may not seem precise,
It shall always come to surface.
That will be a day,
Truly to cherish,
A final moment of truth,
When a witting minds all perish.
And in the end all shall know,
Because of purposes,
Lives do glow.
Oh what a feeling,
All so nice,
To know you've had a purpose,
Is to have lived a good life.

The Troopers That All Died That Day

The troopers that all died that day,
Were a loyal bunch with pride I would say.
They fought until the bitter end,
And side by side, their hearts would never sway.

They served their country well,
Giving all they had.
With loved ones far away,
Their hearts were sometimes sad.

They all had started together,
That day they swore they'd fight.
Just teenagers in age,
Now as men, they knew no fright.

They knew they had a mission,
They knew they had to succeed.
For with freedom in the world,
They'd help to plant a new seed.

Now they were men,
As they battled close together.
Now they were men,
And turn back they could never.

And then there came a shot!
And then there came a cry!
All the troops turned,
To see who was first to die.

Quickly again they all turned,
And charged straight ahead,
Remembering their oaths,
Their lives they would all pledge.

That was the day, those troopers all died.
That was the day their families and friends
all cried.
But yet they still were proud,
For those troopers fought so well that day,
Fighting for a cause,

Freedom all the way!

A Christmas Story

It was a cold day in December,
The snow fell all so high.
All the traffic seemed to stop,
And no one could pass by.

No one could go anywhere,
It seemed the snow was much too high.
So people stayed in their homes,
No planes were scheduled to fly.

I got caught in traffic,
Which seemed to stand too still.
And then I had a thought,
Which gave my heart a thrill.

When Christ was born this day,
It must have been the same,
Everything had stopped,
For the glory of His name.

And then I looked to the sky,
As the evening quickly came.
And then I saw the stars,
And praised His holy name!

And then came help to tow me,
For my car no longer ran.
I then remembered a great story,
I had learned from a dear friend.

It was a story of Three Kings,
Which had traveled to no end.

They had come to praise the Lord,
Each to offer a gift.
I smiled as I looked at the three towers,
Which had come to give me a lift.

Whatever It Takes

Whatever it takes,
Labor or pain.
Whatever it takes,
Throughout the storms and rain,
I shall praise my Lord my God,
And never in vain.

Whatever it takes,
to bring the lost to Christ,
whatever it takes,
I shall do the job,
And do it right.

Should Of , Would Of, Could Of

Should of, would of, could of,
That's what they all say.
But the matter of the fact is, they lost anyway.

Should of, could of would of, It's a game we
all play. But do we realize, the danger of this
game?

Should of, would of, could of. An easy
phrase to say, but what was going to happen
in this life, was going to happen anyway.

Should of, would of, could of,
Please find something else to say.

I've Been Dreaming

I've been dreaming of a time,
When things all would be fine.
No more wars and confusion.
A time of love,
A time of peace,
Where angered hearts were cease.

I've been dreaming of a day,
When hate would go away,
No one lost,
Everything was okay.
And the whole world knew,
Thanks to God above,
There was a better way.

I've been dreaming of love,
I've been dreaming of peace.
I've been dreaming for so long.
But one day I know,
My dream will come true,
And life will be as a song.

Where men and women,
Boys and girls,
Will live and know right from wrong.

I've been dreaming all day,
My thoughts shall never stray.

Some how this life will get much better.
And everyone will know,
That through this life we grow,
And learn to trust in one another.

Each night that I sleep,
I constantly weep.
It seems that problems,
Are always on my shoulders,
I then turn to my wife,
And say why worship life,
And then I begin to hold her.

One day I know,
That through my pains I'll grow.
So I just keep going on.

Through my dreams I keep getting strong.
Knowing that I'll find a way,
I've been dreaming all day long.

The Calling

When the Father calls you,
And He calls but one time.
His decision has been made,
And He has thrown you a line.

If you drop that line,
And fall into high waters,
Remember to swim and pray,
For your sons and daughters.

Believe in God and give all you can,
And you may in the future,
Find you're still in his plan.

For you've got a calling,
From one greater than man.

A Point in Life

There's a point in life
Where we reach our limits,
When we no longer give in,
To society's gimmicks.

When we've decided to end,
The farcity which we beface,
And end all the travesties,
Of our simple disgrace.

There's point in life,
Where we stand and are counted.
When we lose our fears and inhibitions,
No matter how deeply they are mounted.

That is the point,
When all should rejoice,
For that's the point in life,
When we've made the right choice.

Voyage

Voyage is to life,
As pain is to strife.
When we fly we voyage,
As we drive we voyage,
When we climb great heights we voyage.
Just to be alive is to voyage.
When we sail we voyage,
When we fail we voyage,
When we win and lose,
Give and choose,
We voyage.
Whether your riding in a car,
Or traveling on a train,
Sailing or flying in an airplane,
You're on a voyage thru space and time,
An endless sort of reign.
Man often voyages two places at a time,
The voyage here on Earth,
and the voyage of the mind.

When Fasting

When fasting, remember to pray,
For strength thru the night,
And power throughout the day.

Don't let the whole world know,
For you'll only make a show,
Of a truly Christian way.

Remember to be festive,
And never one day gripe,
For when you fast for the Lord,
You always gain a stripe.

Always be strong,
And give all you've got.
For when you've fasted for the Lord,
You've gained a lot.

No one should know you hunger,
Except the Lord above,
No one should know your reasons,
Though the only should be love.

Never criticize those who follow your ways,
For when others follow you,
They're lengthening their days.

Jesus Is Coming

Jesus is coming,
And it won't be long.
We've done some right things,
And we've done some wrong.

It may not be tonight,
It may not be tomorrow,
But Jesus is coming,
So you'd better be strong.

We know not the day.
We know not the hour.
We know not the time,
But we know of his power.

Jesus is coming,
So you'd better get right.
You'd better not lose Him,
Hold on real tight.

It may be tonight,
It may be tomorrow.
but Jesus is coming,
So you'd better get right.

Love one another,
And give all you can.
Pray for the strength,
To fulfill His plan.

For Jesus is coming,
And in Him you'll find a friend.

Be Strong

Be strong all you Christians,
And live each day as the last.
Be strong all you Christians,
And remember our painful past.

Be strong as you walk,
The streets of sin each day.
Be strong as Satan approaches you,
In every kind of way.

Be strong in your marriage.
Be strong in your goals.
Be strong all you Christians,
Young and old.

Be strong when you speak,
for you speak with high authority.
Be strong all you Christians,
And remember your priority.

Be strong as troubles come your way,
Be strong as your adversaries,
Attempt to tackle you as prey.

Be strong and fight,
As if there is no tomorrow,
Be strong all you Christians,
And learn to except sorrow.

Be strong and move on,
To whatever you must achieve.
Be strong all you Christians,
And you shan't be deceived.

Help Them

Help them to understand,
What is to become of man.
Help them to find out,
What Christ is all about.

Help them to live,
Through problems which never seem to end.
Help them to see,
That in Christ we have a friend.

Help them to grow.
Each day, each night and hour.
Help them my friend,
For through Christ you have the power.

Help them learn to pray,
That the Father walks their way.
Help them my friend,
And from this mission,
Never sway.

Help them.

Let Your Light Shine

Let your light shine,
And others shall see
The Lord's great beauty,
All so divine.

A city on a hill,
Can never be hid.
Neither do people light candles,
Only to place them under a lid.

So let your light shine,
Never keep it hid.
For if others don't see the light,
For a Christian happy life,

They can never bid.

Our Parents

Our parents are an example
For all the world to see.
How God's great love for us,
Can set lost hearts so free.

Our parents sometimes must punish us,
Whenever we do wrong,
Through our greatest tribulations,
They must always remain head strong.

Our parents must set an example,
For we small ones to follow.
For one day we shall be as they,
Yes I'm talking about tomorrow.

And remember that when we're spanked,
It serves to teach us a lesson.
Our parents do truly love us,
And of that, there is no question.

Remember when you leave them,
And live life on your own.
You can always go to see them,
Or sometimes call on the telephone.

Remember to always honor them,
Forever and ever more,
It is because they truly love you.
Your bottom has grown so sore.

The New Day

The new day shall come,
When all the world knows His name.
The new day shall come.
When again Christ shall reign.

And all over the vast and open plains,
There shall be food for everyone,
And always enough rain.

There shall be no more wars,
For Satan will have died.
There shall be no more whores,
For men shall all have their brides.

This new day I speak of,
Is approaching us with each hour.
As men and women all over the world,
Learn of His name and power.

And that will be the day truly to rejoice,
When we shall all commune together,
For we will have made the right choice.

The Heirs of Christ

There's a new breed of people,
Which grow stronger each day,
No matter how they stand in society,
For them tomorrow's a better day.

They are the heirs of Christ,
Which inherit all of His love.
They know the wages of sin,
And the power from above.

Some are weak,
Some are strong.
Some of them are poor,
But none could go wrong.

They've inherited much more,
Than life could ever offer,
They've inherited God's love,
And they shall always prosper.

They know that in this life,
All things shall one day end.
They are the heirs of Christ,
And their powers shall transcend.

They may in society.
Never fit the bill.
But they are heirs of Christ,
Through His loving will.

You can be an heir of Christ,
But first you must believe.
In the power of His love,
To the greatest of all degrees.

You too can inherit,
The power of His love.
You too can share,
This greatness from above.

Believe in God with all your heart.
Bring Christ into your life,
And you'll gain a new start.

There is no higher award,
So please listen close my friends,
To be an heir of Christ,
You must be born again.

The War

The war was long,
And many died.
The leaders sought peace,
But they had too much pride.

As the days grew longer,
And the famine grew wide,
The world was soon to learn,
All their leaders had lied.

They had forgotten about Christ,
And the power of love.
They had forgotten revelations,
And that all good things come from above.

And then came disease,
In a hurrisome flurry.
They were losing their minds,
And their eye sights were blurry.

The water supply had dropped below level,
And it was easy to see,
It was the work of the devil,
Finally set free.

And then men and women,
Finally learned to pray.
Though a little too late,
It seemed the only way.

In the midst of the war,
Everyone grew still.
There was a sudden burst light in the sky!
That was sure to kill.

Nuclear bombs were exploding all over.
Women and children were dying,
And their men were not sober.

It seemed that the end,
Had finally come.
Christians sang songs,
And they all sang as one.

And then as the fires,
Began to decline,
People wandering all over,
Most half out their minds.

Then came another great burst,
Which lit up the sky.
Now it was too late to wonder,
What if and why?

Those that survived,
Were the children of Christ.
Those that all died,
Were all caught up in vice.

And for those who knew the Lord,
A new day was to begin.
For those who battle with Satan,
With the Lord at their side,
Are sure to win!

A Life Without Christ

A life without Christ,
Is like a life without hope.
Full of sin and contradictions,
Where there's no room for growth.

A Life without Christ,
Is a life which is lonely,
It's just you alone,
And just you only.

You may have friends and family.
But they are not forever.
You may have material gains.
But save you they can never.

A life without Christ,
Is like a soldier without a weapon,
No armor for protection,
And no means of enemy detection.

A life without Christ,
Is a life without meaning,
No reason to seek answers,
And no reasons for dreaming,
Only problems so demeaning.
A life without Christ,
Is nothing.

Put on Your Coat of Armor

Put on your coat of armor,
As you battle Satan day today.
Never remove your armor,
Or from His grace you'll surely stray.

Don't forget your breastplate,
Your helmet or your sword.
Don't forget the power you have,
When you serve Christ the Lord.

Satan can never harm you,
Or cause your life to change.
For when you wear Christ's coat of armor,
Almighty power comes your way.

The helmet is your salvation,
The breastplate, keeps your heart safe.
The shield protects you from evil,
And the sword are the words you say.

Always stand tall and ready,
As you prepare to battle evil.
Always be ready,
For there can be no retrieval.
Put on your coat of armor,

And you can never lose.
For to serve Christ the Father,
Is to bring the world good news.

The World As I See It

The world as I see it,
Is nearing its fate.
There's no room for argument,
Or even debate.

Politicians keep pushing,
Taxes real high.
Money going to rebels,
At record level highs.

Drugs just like fashions,
In an ongoing trend.
And to be successful in this world,
You can't have a friend.

Our water polluted,
What could be next?
A disease called AIDS,
And everyone must fret.

Ghettoes which do nothing,
But steadily grow.
While suburbs get smaller,
Our stupidity continues to show.

The world as I see it,
Has only one hope.
That Christ return soon,
As the antidote.

I Cast My Thoughts Upon The Waters

*I cast my thoughts upon the waters, past all
the worlds son's, and daughters.
I found a light as I crossed this old world,
I've seen a lot in men in women, in crying
boys and girls.*

*I've learned to except, the things I cannot
change. I've learned to trust in God, for
everything, He'll arrange.*

*I cast my thoughts upon the waters, knowing my
God is able.
I shall not fear my enemies, for with God at
my back, I walk tall, and I am stable.*

*I shall no longer worry, of the simple
things in life, for the Bible told me this
world, would be full of hate and strife.*

*I cast my thoughts upon the waters, and you
should cast yours too. For if you knew the
God that I serve, He would make your life like
new!*

Standing Trial

We all must one day,
Stand before our Maker.
It will be a great day,
But for some, a heartbreaker.

We all must give testimony,
Of the roles we've played in life.
We all must stand trial,
We all must testify.

There will be no judge and jury,
No spectators in fury.
Only you and your maker,
There could be no greater.

You can't run,
And you can't hide.
And by the rules of your trial,
You must abide.

You will each have your chance,
To explain you case.
But remember one thing,
You can easily be disgraced.

If you're innocent,
Stand tall and steady.
If you are guilty,
You'd better get ready.

And as you look into the history,
And see your past.
Remember you were warned,
Where Satan would be cast.

Redeem yourselves now,
In the eyes of God.
And in His courtroom,
You shant have, to feel His rod.
Remember these things when you're on trial,
Standing before God.

We Are the Christians

We are the strong,
And we walk steady.
We are the meek,
Humble and ready.

We are God in action,
You and I.
For we do our jobs willingly,
And we never ask why.

We pray for the world,
Day and night.
We even pray for our enemies,
In God's forgiving sight.

We pray for the leaders,
Which seek freedom and peace.
We pray for the day,
When poverty shall cease.

We pray that tomorrow,
The world will find a way,
To open up its hearts,
Which mostly looks grey.

We are the strong,
And we constantly pray,
Gaining great powers,
Through our prayers day to day.

If you've found the Lord,
That you've searched for to all lengths,
Then you are also a Christian,
With great powers and strength.

We are the Christians,
Men and women, boys and girls,
And we are the light,
Which brightens this lost world.
We are the Christians.

A Childless Heart

A childless heart, is a heart with no feeling
No care for life, only care for the thrilling.

A childless heart, has no morals or being,
just a lost poor soul, without the true gift
of seeing.

A childless heart, knows not of God, just a
wanderer through life, which only dreams of
the odd.

A childless heart is one, which agrees to
killing. They care for no one, the thought
is just chilling!

A true child of God, respects true love and
labor, they are not mislead, by hate, and
hearsayer's.

A childless heart, is one which needs much
attention, lost in a world, which only has
one dimension.

A childless heart, is one that doesn't care.
A childless heart, is one that needs prayer.

Time Is a Passing

Time is a passing,
Where are you going?
The clock is a ticking,
But there is always time for growing.

Time is a passing,
Are things getting better?
Time is a passing,
Even as you read this letter.

Time is a passing,
What are you now doing?
Take a good look at your life,
Is it time for renewing?

Time is a passing,
So you'd better get going.
Time is a passing,
And the glass still is flowing.

Time is a passing,
As Satan continues to grow bolder.
Time is a passing.
And yes your getting older!

Time is passing,
Don't let it pass you by.

Thank You Lord

Thank you Lord,
For opening my eyes.
To the ways of this world,
Full of sin and the unwise.

Thank you Lord,
For giving me a chance,
To come humbly to my knees,
Before the last dance.

Thank you Lord,
For the power that you have given me.
For now I know that I am great,
There is no need for envy.

Thank you Father,
For allowing me to be a part,
Of the greatest body ever.
The body of Jesus Christ,
And the church which is His heart.

Thank you Lord,
For answering my prayers,
For helping me find the happiness,
I knew was always there.

Thank you Lord.

Mountains Were Made to Climb

Mountains were made to climb,
So come and climb with me my friend.
But remember in that climb,
There may be pains which never seem to end.

Mountains were made to climb,
As birds were made to fly.
Remember that in life,
Until the day you die.

Problems which come in life,
Are like the ledges of cliff's.
After conquering each ledge,
It gives your life a lift.

Sometimes you may even fall,
So remember to hold the line,
For you will gain another chance,
To complete your upper climb.

And when you reach the top,
Success was not just a dream.
It will seem your life has a purpose,
And your heart will utterly scream.

So problems were made to conquer,
As mountains were made to climb.
Remember that one fact,
And success I'm sure you'll find.

Christt Is Here

Christ is here!
Don't look to your rear.
Christ is here,
And I do not mean near.

Christ is here,
Just search in your heart,
Christ is here,
So let the rejoicing start.

Christ is in the church,
Christ is in the home,
Christ is all around the world,
Even in Rome.

Christ has never left us,
Since He rose from Calvary.
Christ has never left us,
Through our sins and misery.

Christ is here,
So let the world cheer!
You can feel His powers,
So close and near.

When we all know His name,
And know of His power,
This world shall see Christ,
And His love, in showers.

As revelation spoke,
And said the day would come,
When all would know His name,
And of His kingdom.

Christ is here,
In everyone's heart.
And for those which do not except Him,
There shall be no new start.

Christ is here!

We're On The Way

We're on the way,
To a new and brighter day.
Where love is never gray,
And hearts don't go astray.
We're on the way ya'll,
We're on the way!
We're on the way,
No time to sit or play,
For love has come our way,
And made our lives gay.
We're on the way ya'll,
We're on the way!
Each and every night we pray,
That love will come your way.
We're on the way ya'll,
We're on the way!
One day I know,
That through love you'll see,
The power of love,
Lonely hearts set free.
We're on the way ya'll,
We're on the way!
No time to look back,
Or sleeping in the sack,
For love has come our way.
We're on the way ya'll,
We're on the way!
We're on the way,
And we'll never go astray,
For love has come our way.
We're on the way!!

Nobody Knows Like I Do

Nobody knows my Lord like I do,
Nobody knows what in life He's shown me,
Not even a few.

Nobody knows how much He has given me.
Nobody knows how or why,
My heart is so free.

Nobody knows my Lord,
Quite like I do.

Nobody knows how many lost hearts,
My Lord has set free.
Nobody knows the greatness of his power,
Which has placed the greatest armies in misery.

Nobody knows where,
After this life they may be going.
Nobody knows but Christ,
And His powers are always showing.

Nobody knows when this world will end.
Nobody knows,
Neither I nor you, my friend.

Nobody knows like I do,
That with Christ as my leader.
Problems in my life,
Are so, so few.

A Message To All Nations

Here is a message, I send to all nations
under God.
Hear me all you leaders of this world
who fear the power of His mighty rod.

You had better learn, how to forgive
and forget, for with wars upon wars, we shall
continue in regret.

This is not a message, to put our leaders down,
but a message sent in love,
and sent from the Highest Crown.

He said it in His word, He said it loud and
clear. Love Him with all of your heart, and
hold your neighbors dear.

That is Gods covenant, and that is Gods cure,
we should love everyone, and our love should be pure.

Whether rich or poor, make peace with your
neighbors, at your front and back door.

And then He shall bless all nations of the
world,
Again it will be safe, for all men
and women, boys and girls.

Stand fast all you leaders, lead in love & compassion.
And you shall make love, like a never ending Fashion.

Wake Up All You Leaders!

Wake up all you leaders,
And remember who you lead.
Remember your oaths of office,
To help your people succeed.

Remember your being watched,
Your in the eyes of the whole wide world.
Try to study war no more, think of the boys
and girls.

Wake up all you leaders, and remember your
campaign speeches.
Stop all of the parties and dinning, with
all of those corporate leeches.

Wake up all you leaders, who hold the world
in your dangerous hands,
Remember you were warned, that Satan would
be banned.

Why Take An Oath And Tell A Lie?

Why take an oath and tell a lie,
leaving the people wondering,
What if and why?

Why tell the people, you promise to lead!
When all the time, your buried in misdeed.

Stealing our dollars, while gaining some
fame. Misleading the people, don't you
know that's insane!

Take a look in the mirror, and see what God sees.
Don't you know you can't hide, and the truth always
frees.

Why take an oath and tell a lie,
have not you heard,
God hears our every cry?

No matter what you do, no matter what
you say. God will save His people,
we'll all see a brighter day!

Why take an oath and tell a lie.
God will one day judge you,
and it will be too late to cry!

A Strong Man Knows

A strong man knows, how to turn the other
cheek. A strong man knows, that love is
not weak.

A strong man knows, that there
is wisdom in struggle, A strong man knows
that with freedom, comes a tuggle.

A strong man knows, that he must fight for his rights,
and in everything he seeks to be,
He must struggle for day and night.

A strong man knows the limits of his strengths,
he knows the abilities he has, and he must
use it at all lengths.

A strong man knows, that to cry is not to be
weak, For Christ one day cried, for
the poor and the meek.

A strong man knows, what it is to be strong,
For he must toil all day long,
with what's right and with what is wrong.

A strong man knows.

Travel A Million Miles

*You can travel a million miles and be back
in one day.
It sounds so hard to do but we do it
everyday!*

*We travel in our minds, to never ending
heights,
Just look how far we've come, through our
dreams and endless sights!*

*Our population has tripled, and we've
traveled to the moon. We we're once just a
people, who lived in a lagoon.*

*We've done so many things, we've traveled
all so far. It seems we could even reach
out, and touch the furthest star.*

*We've created great and awesome empires,
that seem like works of art.
But that too will end, and we'll be right
back at the start.*

*For we are only temporary.
Remember that and be smart!*

True Freedom

Mankind can be free and yet imprisoned by
so many things,
think of all of our, battles,
all of the arrows and the slings!

We battle with more, than municipalities in
high places, more than with substance abuse
and ethical races.

And yet we cry for freedom for ourselves and the world,
Freedom of choice for our boys and girls.
Do we really know what freedom really is?
Could we answer if given a quiz?

Do we have the power to just say no?
To unjust behavior by our leaders and foe?
Can we live without fear of attack,
and can we live without turning our back?

With so many questions, it seems hard to
write this poem, living in a country
with the essence of early Rome.

True freedom to many, is our countries
present state,
but if you'd look to the scriptures,
You'd find room for debate!

Colours Of the Heart

Colours of the heart, are like the awesome
colors in a rainbow, So many beautiful
colors, and all with a special glow!

Some are shades of white, some are shades of
gray, but most are shades of happiness which
gleam more, day by day.

Colours of the heart are like the
millions of thoughts in the mind,
and the steady beat of a vessel,
Which knows no such thing as time.

Colours of the heart are like the
colours in the sea, so many beautiful creatures,
 living in a world so free.

The colours of the heart are the
colors of you and me, thank God for these
beautiful colors, a beauty the world can see.

The Mansion by the Sea

There is a mansion that I know of, which sits
by the sea, if you ever get to visit, it is
because you've been set free.

In this mansion which I speak of,
there are many separate rooms.
It is never over crowded, and no such
thing as arriving too soon!

In this mansion which I speak of,
You too can partner in,
there isn't much to invest,
for through His mercy and grace,
He's forgiven your every sin.

There is always someone to welcome you,
for this is a mansion of love.
There are always choruses singing,
Singing to God above.

Don't you worry about eating,
for here there is food for life.
This is a home where there is no suffering,
a home where there is no strife.

If you are blessed you'll get to visit
,this awesome home of Christ!
Remember you where promised, of
this Victory in sight!

C' Est La Vie

C'est La Vie my friend,
It's time for us to part,
though I knew we would, right from the start.

C'est La Vie, parting is such sweet sorrow,
C'est La Vie my friend, there shall be no
tomorrow.

C'est La Vie you cruel, cruel world.
I go to meet my Maker, for in Gods great
heart, we are all just boys and girls.

C'est La Vie, shall I see you again?
Only if God wishes, and in Christ you have a
friend.

C'est La Vie my friend, I'm finally going
home, no more in this evil world,
shall I be forced to roam.

Though leaving is such sweet, sweet
sorrow,
Please do not weep,
for me there is a greater tomorrow,
in the greatness of my sleep.

C' Est La Vie.

Listen to the True Sounds Of Life

Listen to the true sounds of life, hear Gods
freedom, without pains and strife.
Listen close my friends,
and hear the true sounds of life.

Listen to the wind, as it sings a special
song, listen and hear life, never old,
always young.

Listen to the birds, as they sing all day
long. Listen to the creatures in life, and
you'll hear a great, great song.

Listen to the thunder, as it plows through
the lightning,
listen close my friend, to a power
that's sometimes frightening.

Listen to the owl, as it speaks to the
night, listen to it howl,
As it causes most to fright.

Listen and you'll know,
there's a greater power than man,
and it will always show.

Listen close my friend, to the true sounds
of life.

Signs of The Times

There are signs of the times, that the
Bible speaks of. There are signs of the
times, which come from God above!

Look at the weather, we cannot predict.
Look at mighty earthly quakes, we never
seem to lick.

Signs of the times are suddenly here.
While we look for explanations,
continue interrogations,
remain loss in our frustrations,
And continue in separation.
We should remember the power
of supplication.

Signs of the times are suddenly here.
But look to God my friend,
and have no need to fear!

The Oprah Winfrey Story

*Her name is Oprah Winfrey, and she heard the
people's cry. So she put together a talk
show, that would tell the reasons why.*

*This woman has made a difference, in millions of
people's lives. She continues to touch the
world, helping millions of singles, husbands
and wives.*

*A philanthropist that's real, and
an artist with true skill. This is a woman
of power, and a woman of true good will.*

*Answering causes in Africa, and all around
the world. God continues to bless her, as
she blesses lost boys and girls.*

*Her name is Oprah Winfrey, and to many she's a hero.
This is a woman of valor, who doesn't know
the meaning of zero.*

Victory's in Sight!

Victory's in sight, so hold your head high,
For we serve a God,
who will hear our every cry!
Victory's in sight, so there's no need to fear,
God will fight your battles,
His angles are always near!

Don't be afraid, to walk in the valley,
For God is at your back.
Don't be afraid, to stand against evil.
For with He, nothing shall you lack!

Remember to stand tall,
when you face your enemy,
For you can never fail.
Remember when you build with the Father,
Your ship will always sail.

Remember the battle of Israel,
When God parted the waters in the sea!
Remember what Moses told Pharaoh.
God's people will surely be free!

Trust in the Lord, believe in His might.
Stand tall as David as he went to war,
and defeated Goliath before the night.

Victory is yours, when you give your life to Christ,
Like Meshach, Shadrach, and Abenego.
You'll withstand the fiery, dungeons of life!
Victory is yours!!!!

My Father Takes me Higher

My Father takes me higher,
To places the eye cannot see.
My Father takes me higher,
With He, I am truly free!

My Father takes me higher,
to serve Him is my only desire.
Of His message I shall act,
As a humble towns crier.
Spreading the news,
That the devil is a liar!

My Father takes me higher,
To wherever I want to be,
Because of His love and compassion,
We hold in our minds the ultimate key!

My Father takes me higher,
And He will take you there too.
Simply fall to your knees,
Acknowledge His love,
And you'll take on a brand new view.

In This Hour

In this hour, thousands shall die,
In this hour, millions shall cry.

In this hour Killings are going on,
In this hour, thousands are singing the same
old song.

In this hour hundreds of thousands
are finding Christ. In this hour, millions of
people all over the world, are gaining a new
lease on life!

In this hour married couples
are fighting, somewhere there is lightning,
and leaders are planning wars, that soldiers
and their loved ones, don't find too exciting.

In this hour, we need more than life has to
give. In this hour we need Christ in our
lives, and our Father who gives. For then
we can begin again, to find a reason to live.

In this hour, my prayer is for you,
That you will find the strength, to keep your life anew

I Want To Be Rich

*I want to be rich, and wear clothing of
royal colors. I want to be rich and regret
it, I will never!*

*I want to move mountains, as though a King
moves mountains all so high,
I want to live in luxury, and never be asked
why?*

*I want to rule my own life, and guide all
others, I want to lead the people of this
world, both fathers and mothers.*

*I want to tell politicians, to hear my
maddening cry, I want to be rich, and never
ever sigh.*

*I want to be rich, in Gods ever loving world,
I want to be rich, To serve my Lords,
 men and women, boys and
girls.*

*I want to be rich, in knowledge of my Lord,
For then I can serve, and truly afford.*